Cognitive-Behavioral Stress Management for Prostate Cancer Recovery

✓ **Treatments** *That Work*™

Cognitive-Behavioral Stress Management for Prostate Cancer Recovery

Facilitator Guide

Frank J. Penedo • Michael H. Antoni • Neil Schneiderman

OXFORD
UNIVERSITY PRESS

2008

OXFORD
UNIVERSITY PRESS

Oxford University Press, Inc., publishes works that further
Oxford University's objective of excellence
in research, scholarship, and education.

Oxford   New York
Auckland   Cape Town   Dar es Salaam   Hong Kong   Karachi
Kuala Lumpur   Madrid   Melbourne   Mexico City   Nairobi
New Delhi   Shanghai   Taipei   Toronto

With offices in
Argentina   Austria   Brazil   Chile   Czech Republic   France   Greece
Guatemala   Hungary   Italy   Japan   Poland   Portugal   Singapore
South Korea   Switzerland   Thailand   Turkey   Ukraine   Vietnam

Published by Oxford University Press, Inc.
198 Madison Avenue, New York, New York 10016

www.oup.com

Oxford is a registered trademark of Oxford University Press

Library of Congress Cataloging-in-Publication Data
Penedo, Frank J.
Cognitive-behavioral stress management for prostate cancer recovery :
facilitator guide / Frank J. Penedo, Michael H. Antoni, Neil Schneiderman.
p. ; cm. — (TreatmentsThatWork)
Includes bibliographical references.
ISBN 978–0–19–533697–9
1. Prostate—Cancer—Patients—Rehabilitation.   2. Prostate—Cancer—
Psychological aspects.   3. Stress management.   4. Cognitive therapy.
5. Relaxation.   I. Antoni, Michael H.   II. Schneiderman, Neil.
III. Title.   IV. Series: Treatments that work.
[DNLM: 1. Stress, Psychological—Prevention.   2. Cognitive
Therapy—methods.   3. Postoperative Complications—psychology.
4. Postoperative Complications—rehabilitation.   5. Prostatectomy—
psychology.   6. Prostatectomy—rehabilitation.   7. Prostatic
Neoplasms—complications.   8. Relaxation Techniques.
WM 172 P398c 2008]
RC280.P7P46   2008
616.99′463—dc22

9   8   7   6   5   4   3   2   1

Printed in the United States of America
on acid-free paper

About Treatments *ThatWork*™

Stunning developments in healthcare have taken place over the last several years, but many of our widely accepted interventions and strategies in mental health and behavioral medicine have been brought into question by research evidence as not only lacking benefit, but perhaps, inducing harm. Other strategies have been proven effective using the best current standards of evidence, resulting in broad-based recommendations to make these practices more available to the public. Several recent developments are behind this revolution. First, we have arrived at a much deeper understanding of pathology, both psychological and physical, which has led to the development of new, more precisely targeted interventions. Second, our research methodologies have improved substantially, such that we have reduced threats to internal and external validity, making the outcomes more directly applicable to clinical situations. Third, governments around the world and healthcare systems and policymakers have decided that the quality of care should improve, that it should be evidence based, and that it is in the public's interest to ensure that this happens (Barlow, 2004; Institute of Medicine, 2001).

Of course, the major stumbling block for clinicians everywhere is the accessibility of newly developed evidence-based psychological interventions. Workshops and books can go only so far in acquainting responsible and conscientious practitioners with the latest behavioral healthcare practices and their applicability to individual patients. This new series, Treatments *ThatWork*™, is devoted to communicating these exciting new interventions to clinicians on the frontlines of practice.

The manuals and workbooks in this series contain step-by-step detailed procedures for assessing and treating specific problems and diagnoses.

But this series also goes beyond the books and manuals by providing an-cillary materials that will approximate the supervisory process in assist-ing practitioners in the implementation of these procedures in their practice.

In our emerging healthcare system, the growing consensus is that evi-dence-based practice offers the most responsible course of action for the mental health professional. All behavioral healthcare clinicians deeply desire to provide the best possible care for their patients. In this series, our aim is to close the dissemination and information gap and make that possible.

This facilitator guide, and the companion workbook for participants, is designed to help men deal with the stress of readjusting to life after sur-gery for prostate cancer. Prostate cancer is the most common cancer (other than skin cancers) in American men, affecting one in six. How-ever, the prognosis for men surgically treated for localized prostate can-cer is overwhelmingly positive.

This group program addresses men's quality of life after treatment. Par-ticipants learn Cognitive-Behavioral Stress Management (CBSM) tech-niques, as well as a variety of relaxation methods. This two-pronged ap-proach is optimal for reducing stress and maintaining overall health. Group discussion and examples speak to having had prostate cancer, adding value to this CBSM program. Those working with this popula-tion will find this guide an invaluable resource.

David H. Barlow, Editor-in-Chief,
Treatments *ThatWork*™
Boston, Massachusetts

References

Barlow, D. H. (2004). Psychological treatments. *American Psychologist, 59,* 869–878.

Institute of Medicine (2001). *Crossing the quality chasm: A new health system for the 21st century.* Washington, DC: National Academy Press.

Contents

Acknowledgments

This facilitator guide and accompanying workbook were developed over several years of theoretical and empirical research conducted in the Behavioral Medicine Research Center at the University of Miami (UM) Department of Psychology and the Sylvester Comprehensive Cancer Center (SCCC). Through a National Cancer Institute (NCI)-funded mind-body center, The Center for Psycho-Oncology Research (CPOR), we brought together an interdisciplinary team of clinical psychologists, oncologists, immunologists, and endocrinologists to examine the effects of stress and stress management on quality of life (QOL) and physical health outcomes among men treated for prostate cancer (PCa). With the support of this NCI center, we were able to develop and deliver the group-based cognitive-behavioral stress management (CBSM) intervention for improving QOL and physical health in an ethnically and socioeconomically diverse group of men treated for PCa. We are indebted to the NCI for these years of support that allowed us to develop a theoretically based and empirically supported CBSM intervention for localized PCa.

We are also thankful to the many faculty, scientists, clinicians, postdocs, and graduate and undergraduate students at the UM and the UM/ SCCC who facilitated the body of research that has been conducted with this intervention. The early developmental work was led by ourselves along with Drs. Jason Dahn, Jeffrey Gonzalez, Suzanne Lechner, and Dean Cruess. We also received considerable guidance from Dr. Bernard Roos, a geriatrician, and Drs. Edward Gheiler and Mark Soloway, urologists. We were fortunate to have a talented group of graduate students who aided considerably in this work including Ivan Molton, Dave Kinsinger, Scott Siegel, and Jose Sandoval. We are also indebted for the contributions by other faculty in our Behavioral Medicine Research

Center and the UM/SCCC including Drs. Ron Duran, Maria Llabre, Charles Carver, MaryAnn Fletcher, Mahendra Kumar, Elizabeth Thomas, and Sharlene Weiss. We also thank Lara Traeger, M.S., one of our current graduate students, who played an instrumental role in the editorial process of putting this guide together. We are also grateful for the editorial assistance provided to us by Julia TerMaat of Oxford University Press.

Finally, we are grateful and indebted to the many men who participated in our randomized clinical trials and provided their valuable time and effort in our research studies. We are fortunate to have worked with such a courageous group of PCa survivors who shared with us their intimate and moving experiences. From them we have learned a great deal about resiliency and survivorship in the face of adversity. Their contribution to our research studies have made this guide possible and we are forever grateful.

Background Information and Purpose of this Program

The Cognitive-Behavioral Stress Management (CBSM) program for prostate cancer (PCa) is a 10-week group-based psychosocial intervention that was adapted from our group's earlier work with men and women living with human immunodeficiency virus (HIV) infection and women treated for breast cancer (BCa). This program was specifically modified for men treated with surgery (e.g., radical prostatectomy) for localized (Stages I/II) PCa. The CBSM program for PCa combines relaxation and cognitive-behavioral techniques to help PCa survivors improve general and disease-specific (e.g., sexual functioning) quality of life. Our CBSM intervention is designed to (a) increase stress awareness by identifying sources of stress and the nature of the stress response; (b) teach anxiety reduction skills such as deep breathing and progressive muscle relaxation; (c) modify negative thought processes and appraisals by teaching cognitive-restructuring skills; (d) build adaptive coping skills and increase emotional expression; (e) increase availability and utilization of social support networks; (f) enhance interpersonal skills through improved communication skills and assertiveness training; and (g) promote health maintenance through reductions in health risk behavior and medical treatment adherence strategies. This CBSM intervention is specifically tailored to address specific issues relevant to men treated for localized PCa including loss of control, treatment side effects (e.g., sexual dysfunction), illness-related spousal/partner disruption, and social isolation.

The CBSM intervention is a 10-week, manualized, and sequenced group-based intervention that meets weekly for 2–2.5 hours. Each session is divided into two segments: a relaxation training segment and a stress management segment. All sessions begin with a relaxation training exercise that involves in-session training and practice of a new relaxation technique. The second segment of the weekly meetings covers stress-management; participants learn cognitive-behavioral techniques that can be applied to address ongoing general and prostate cancer-related stressors (e.g., spousal/partner disruption, sexual dysfunction, navigating the medical system). Although other available programs target cognitive-behavioral and relaxation strategies to address PCa concerns, unlike other programs our CBSM intervention is designed to be conducted in groups of six to eight men led by one or two group facilitators. This format provides several unique features to facilitate adjustment and improve quality of life in men treated for localized PCa. By participating in a group with other men who have had similar illness-related experiences, participants develop a sense of commonality and a connection with other men that facilitates learning and sharing of information. Furthermore, group leaders draw from the experiences of the participants and develop a supportive group environment where they (a) commonly serve as coping role models along with the participants and foster positive social comparisons, (b) encourage emotional expression and provide the opportunity to experience social support, (c) assist participants in replacing feelings of uncertainty and develop a sense of self-confidence, and (d) discourage maladaptive coping (avoidance, denial), and encourage adaptive (acceptance, positive reframing) coping responses. More information on the logistics of the group program is provided in chapter 2 of this guide.

Problem Focus

Prostate cancer is the most commonly diagnosed non-skin carcinoma. Most PCa cases are diagnosed at the localized stage (Stage I/II), when the tumor is confined to the prostate capsule. Therefore, survival rates for localized disease are very high, with some estimates approaching 100% survival at 5 years post-treatment (ACS, 2007). Radical prostatectomy (RP; surgical removal of the prostate gland) and external beam radiotherapy (EBR) are the most widely used treatments for localized disease followed by hormone therapy and watchful waiting. Treatment options for PCa are often determined by cancer stage, tumor size, and prostate-specific antigen (PSA) level, as well as the age, health status, and preference of the individual at the time of diagnosis. Despite high survival rates, available treatments for PCa lead to significant acute and chronic side effects (e.g., sexual, urinary, and bowel dysfunction), which can compromise quality of life (QOL; Potosky et al., 2004). At 2 years after treatment, 82% of RP patients and 50% of EBR patients have erectile dysfunction (ED). After 5 years the adjusted percentages for RP and EBR are 79% and 64%, respectively. In terms of urinary function the proportion of men reporting lack of total urinary control after RP is about 79% at 6 months and 68% by 2 years (Stanford et al., 2000). Whereas many fewer EBR than RP patients are urinary incontinent soon after treatment as well as 5 years later (e.g., 15% RP vs. 4% EBR), men who receive EBR tend to show greater difficulty with obstructive symptoms such as slow urination and urinary urgency (Potosky et al., 2004).

A recent evaluation of the impact of treatment-related dysfunction on more global QOL demonstrated that men with urinary or sexual dysfunction, or both, demonstrate significant decrements in multiple QOL domains (including bodily pain, mental health, emotional role, physical role, vitality, and health status [Penson et al., 2003]). Furthermore, other work suggests that up to 30% of men diagnosed with localized PCa may report clinically significant levels of psychological distress and that such distress is typically associated with sexual and urinary dysfunction, and fear of recurrence (Schover et al., 2002; Wei et al., 2002; Zabora et al., 2001). Therefore, a PCa survivor's ability to sustain a relatively adequate level of QOL and overall adjustment following treatment may to some extent depend on his ability to adaptively face and engage the multiple challenges (e.g., treatment side effects) encountered. It has been documented that factors such as supportive social networks, accurate cognitive appraisals, and adaptive coping strategies are significantly associated with overall positive adjustment and lower levels of depression and anxiety post PCa treatment. That is, PCa survivors with supportive family and friends, and less intrusive thoughts about cancer (Lepore & Helgeson, 1998), as well as those showing a greater capacity to engage in adaptive coping strategies such as active-behavioral (planning, seeking social support) or active-cognitive (acceptance, finding meaning in an illness, reframing) coping have reported better overall adjustment (Ptacek, Pierce, Ptacek, & Nogel, 1999). Finally, one must consider that because

PCa is predominantly a disease of older men, with about 70% of cases diagnosed in men over age 64, normal age-related physical changes, as well as other comorbid conditions, may compound treatment-related side effects and further compromise overall QOL.

Development of this Treatment Program

Over the past 20 years, our group has systematically evaluated the effects of stress management interventions in HIV infection, breast cancer, chronic fatigue, cardiovascular disease, and more recently, PCa (Antoni, Schneiderman, & Penedo, 2007). We developed our CBSM program for localized PCa based on the rationale that while treatment for localized disease is highly successful, persistent and often debilitating treatment side effects, as well as ongoing disease status monitoring (i.e., PSA testing) can present the PCa survivors with a series of chronic challenges that can compromise QOL and overall well-being. Based on a chronic disease model, we propose that the extent to which CBSM modifies emotional distress, maladaptive coping, negative appraisals, and social isolation in the context of coping with PCa treatment-related side effects, the intervention program may also positively impact general and disease-specific QOL, emotional well-being, and overall adjustment.

The development of our intervention program for PCa is based on available empirical studies conducted in localized PCa which suggest that a host of psychosocial factors are associated with QOL in this population (e.g., Eton & Lepore, 2002; Schover et al., 2002; Balderson & Towell, 2003). Based on these observations and our prior work, we developed an intervention model that reflects our findings and suggests that a CBSM intervention in men treated for localized PCa (a) improves overall QOL; (b) enhances stress management skills (e.g., ability to engage in adaptive coping and correct negative thinking); (c) improves positive outlook and benefit finding (BF); and (d) among distressed and anxious participants improves emotional well-being and sexual functioning, respectively (Penedo et al., 2002; 2004a,b; 2006; 2003; Molton et al., 2007; Traeger et al, 2007). Collectively, our CBSM intervention program shows that men treated for localized disease can derive multiple benefits by participating in a group-based stress management intervention.

Our CBSM studies in localized PCa show that the CBSM intervention significantly improves overall QOL among CBSM participants relative to men participating in a 1-day control condition seminar that covers stress management skills. We also identified a mechanism through which the CBSM intervention improves QOL. A measure of perceived stress management skills (PSMS), developed to assess an individual's perceived competence in exercising a range of stress management skills, mediated the relationship between group assignment and QOL and remained a significant predictor of post-intervention QOL. Our findings suggest that the intervention had an impact on men's overall QOL such that these improvements were mediated by men's perceived ability to utilize stress management skills. This improvement was not related to ethnic group membership. Our CBSM intervention in PCa has been successfully delivered to an ethnically and economically diverse group of men, including Spanish-monolingual participants. Although non-Hispanic white participants reported significantly better QOL than Latino/Hispanic or African-American participants at baseline, there was no evidence that the CBSM intervention was effective differentially for any one ethnic group. This suggests that our CBSM intervention adequately addressed the QOL needs and properly targeted stress-management skills in an ethnically diverse sample of men treated for PRCA. We have found that the CBSM intervention also improves BF. Work in other cancer populations has begun to document the possibility that for some patients, the experience of cancer may result in positive psychological benefits and actually promote both better emotional well-being and physiological outcomes (e.g., reduced cortisol output; Cruess, Antoni, McGregor et al., 2000; Antoni, Lehman, Kilbourn et al., 2001). We reported that participation in our CBSM program was associated with significant improvements in both QOL and BF. Moreover, the relationship between group assignment and QOL and BF was also mediated by CBSM-associated changes in perceived stress management skills (PSMS), suggesting that skills gained through participation in our intervention explained the increases observed in our outcomes. Separate analyses also indicated that men appear to have enhanced coping skills and reduced distress as a result of our CBSM intervention, as our findings have also showed that participation in the CBSM group was significantly associated with reductions in denial coping and negative mood and improvements in positive reframing.

In addition to significant improvements in general QOL, coping, BF, and perceived stress management skills, and reductions in negative mood, our CBSM intervention has shown significant improvements in sexual and urinary function. We have found that anxiety moderates the intervention's effect on the sexual functioning scores of surgery participants. After controlling for pre-intervention sexual functioning, we showed that CBSM participants with high anxiety showed significant improvements in sexual functioning relative to a comparison group of men who participated in an only 1-day seminar and showed no improvement in sexual functioning over the 12-week follow-up period. We have also shown that among our surgery participants regardless of anxiety levels, participation in our CBSM intervention is associated with statistically and clinically significant increases in sexual functioning. Participants in our CBSM intervention showed significant improvements from baseline to post-CBSM intervention in sexual functioning. It is worth noting that these effects were only identified among our surgery participants. From our work in localized prostate cancer, we have identified that our EBR participants are older (70 yr. vs. 60 yr. for surgery) and report lower socioeconomic status (SES) and a longer time since treatment. Radiation participants also reported more comorbidities and were more likely to be taking antihypertensives and antidepressants. These differences could explain the lack of effects of CBSM on sexual functioning among patients treated with EBR. We have also demonstrated that the intervention has a significant impact on the urinary functioning scores of surgery patients such that the mean pre-post intervention urinary functioning scores of CBSM participants increase relative to men not participating in the CBSM program. Finally, we also documented the efficacy of the intervention in improving emotional well-being among participants who reported high levels of perceived stress on entry into the study. Moreover, we showed that such CBSM-associated improvements in emotional well-being were mediated by changes in illness perceptions. Specifically, changes in perceived treatment control and illness coherence partially mediated the relationship between CBSM group assignment and post-intervention levels of emotional well-being. Throughout this research program, we have consistently found that this 10-week group-based CBSM intervention can positively impact multiple outcomes and significantly improve adjustment among PCa survivors. Our findings suggest that while CBSM improves overall QOL, BF, coping skills, mood, and perceived stress management skills for men treated with surgery or EBR, this work also shows that CBSM's impact on sexual functioning is limited to men treated with surgery or men reporting high levels of anxiety and interpersonal deficits. Similarly, CBSM's effects on overall emotional well-being are limited to men reporting high levels of perceived stress. Therefore, men reporting significant levels of psychosocial distress and interpersonal difficulties may derive the most benefit in terms of disease-specific (e.g., sexual functioning) QOL and overall emotional well-being by participating in this program.

What Is CBSM for Localized PCa?

The CBSM intervention for localized PCa is a program that integrates relaxation, stress management, and health promotion theory into practice by means of providing a comprehensive 10-week program aimed at improving QOL and adjustment among PCa survivors. This program brings together various types of relaxation (Berstain & Borkivec, 1973), imagery, and other anxiety reduction techniques coupled with widely used and validated cognitive-behavioral approaches such as cognitive restructuring (Beck & Emory, 1979), coping skills training (Folkman et al., 1991), communication skills, assertiveness training, and anger management (Ironson et al., 1989). The techniques presented over the 10-week intervention period are specifically tailored to meet the needs of PCa survivors and thus improve their QOL by increasing stress awareness, teaching anxiety reduction skills, modifying distorted cognitive appraisals, building coping skills, reducing social isolation, and enhancing communication skills.

Other Intervention Strategies for PCa

Psychosocial interventions specifically tailored to meet the needs of cancer patients include supportive-expressive group therapy (Spiegel & Yalom, 1978), psychoeducational interventions, and multimodal intervention approaches (Fawzy, Fawzy, Hyun, et al., 1993; Fawzy et al., 1997). Research shows that effective therapy components in multimodal efforts include relaxation training (e.g., guided imagery) to lower arousal; disease information and management; an emotionally supportive environment where participants can address fears and anxieties; behavioral and cognitive coping strategies; and social support (Andersen, 1992). Several reviews describe the efficacy of psychosocial interventions among cancer patients (Meyer & Mark, 1995). Our CBSM intervention model is based on these multimodal approaches delivered in a supportive group environment where 6–8 men meet once a week over a 10-week period with two group leaders facilitating the intervention. Nonetheless, other intervention programs have shown some beneficial effects among PCa survivors.

Mishel et al. (2002) has shown that a psychoeducational intervention delivered over the telephone that teaches cognitive and coping strategies (e.g., cognitive reframing, problem solving) and patient-provider communication skills, and provides medical information, can successfully improve cognitive processing and problem solving among a multiethnic and diverse SES sample of PCa survivors. Therefore, whereas our program provides a face-to-face group format to provide relaxation and stress management skills, other delivery modalities for similar interventions may provide some benefits to PCa survivors. Our group is in the process of conducting a feasibility study of a telephone-delivered version of CBSM to men living with advanced PCa. We reasoned that a home-based delivery system would be more feasible because this population is likely to be older and have more comorbid conditions and functional limitations.

Other psychosocial interventions in PCa have involved social support and psychoeducational interventions which have shown some promise. For example, Gregoire et al. (1997) reported that men who participated in a supportive group had a better understanding of their illness, perceived themselves as more involved in their treatment, felt reassured sharing their experiences with others, and had less anxiety and a more positive outlook. In one study evaluating the efficacy of psychosocial interventions in PCa, Lepore & Helgeson (1998) tested the extent to which patients participating in a support group developed self-efficacy through direct education or social sharing, and lowered cancer-related distress by targeting intrusive thoughts with the support of peers. Men in the 6-week intervention condition had greater improvements in mental health, fewer interpersonal conflicts, larger increases in perceived control over health, and lower distress associated with cancer intrusive thoughts. The intervention was especially beneficial to men with inadequate social resources and low social support from family and friends (Eton, Lepore, & Helgeson, 2001); however, the sample was limited to non-Hispanic white men. In a separate study, Lepore et al. (2003) randomized men recently treated for PCa to a control group, a group-based education intervention (GE), or group-based education plus discussion (GED). The 6-week study significantly increased PCa-specific knowledge in the GE and GED groups relative to control group, and reduced sexual bother was also observed in the GED group. For non-college graduates, both group interventions resulted in better physical functioning scores, and the GED group also reported more positive health behaviors. While there were no overall changes in distress or QOL, this is not surprising given the information-provision focus of the intervention. The results suggest that other interventions with an educational component may be particularly salient for men with less education and possibly limited access to health care information.

Outline of this Treatment Program

The overall aims, general strategies, and specific techniques of the 10-week program are summarized in Table 1.1. Fidelity checklists are included in an appendix and can be photocopied. Each checklist includes an outline of the corresponding session and space for recording time units. Facilitators may want to use these as part of the supervision process or to rate self-adherence.

This CBSM program uses five sets of stress management techniques: cognitive restructuring, coping skills training, assertiveness training, anger management, and social support strategies. About 1–3 weeks are dedicated to training participants in the use of each of these strategies. Each week over the 10-week period a new topic is presented with background

Table 1.1 CBSM Components and Strategies

Aim 1.	**Increase Stress Awareness**	• Identify components of the stress response by focusing on the psychological and physiological responses to stress. • Identify frequently occurring stressors and signs of the stress response. • Understand the experience of tension in the body.
Aim 2.	**Teach Anxiety-Reduction Skills**	• Provide multiple relaxation techniques to reduce anxiety and tension (PMR, deep breathing, autogenics, meditation). • Achieve a sense of mastery over stressors. • Aim to "take the edge off" acute emotional and somatic responses.
Aim 3.	**Modify Cognitive Appraisals**	• Modify appraisals of stressful events. • Use cognitive restructuring and rational thought replacement. • Identify links between thoughts, emotions, and bodily changes. • Enhance familiarity with commonly used distorted thoughts. • Identify steps to replace distortions with rational interpretations.
Aim 4.	**Build Coping Skills and Increase Emotional Expression**	• Challenge and change cognitive, behavioral, and interpersonal coping strategies. • Increase awareness of use of maladaptive ways of coping with stress. • Replace less efficient and indirect ways of coping with direct emotion- and problem-focused strategies. • Increase expression of feelings in response to a stressful situation. • Increase awareness of angry responses and external/internal triggers. • Provide assertiveness and communication skills training and teach anger management.
Aim 5.	**Reduce Social Isolation**	• Identify and use beneficial sources of social support. • Process perceived satisfaction with available social networks. • Identify sources of emotional, financial, and guidance support. • Provide support for others. • Understand the "stress buffering" role of emotional support. • List potential obstacles to maintaining a strong support network.
Aim 6.	**Reduce Risk Behavior and Enhance Treatment Adherence**	• Modify patient beliefs by providing information provision and cognitive restructuring. • Target intentions for health maintenance through motivational enhancement training. • Change negative habits by stimulus control and self-monitoring strategies. • Address barriers to health maintenance through coping skills training. • Enhance physician-patient relations through assertiveness training and coping skills training.

information and in-session exercises. This approach assists participants in increasing their awareness of subtle stress responses that are addressed by the technique being presented. Once a topic is introduced, the facilitators present the rationale for the technique and steps for implementing it. Throughout the remainder of the session, participants are encouraged to discuss ongoing stressors in their lives and how to apply the new stress management technique. This is facilitated through role-playing exercises and breakaways, as well as dyads to maintain the interactive nature of the group experience. Weekly homework assignments are provided to reinforce the techniques presented in each session.

In addition to the stress management topics, the CBSM program provides participants with a set of relaxation exercises that includes progressive muscle relaxation (PMR), deep breathing, guided imagery, autogenic training, diaphragmatic breathing, and various forms of meditation. Most of the relaxation scripts provided in this guide are simplified versions of relaxation methods that are widely used and well validated. Facilitators may want to review full-length versions of many of these procedures in *The Relaxation & Stress Reduction Workbook* (Davis, Eshelman & McKay, 1988), *Hypnosis for Change, 3rd Ed.* (Hadley and Staudacher, 1996), *Guide to Stress Reduction* (Mason, 1986), and *Full Catastrophe Living* (Kabat-Zinn, 1990). The program is designed to have each session introduce either a new technique or a more complex version of a previously introduced relaxation exercise. At the beginning of each session, the group leaders present and review the rationale and steps for carrying out the relaxation technique with the group members. The major part of the relaxation segment of each session is dedicated to having the participants practice the relaxation exercise. Following each exercise, the participants have an opportunity to discuss their experiences. Facilitators then instruct participants to perform the relaxation techniques on their own at least once a day. This format is designed to present the participants over a 10-week period a set of relaxation exercises and skills that they can import into and practice in their home environments. By providing several different techniques, participants will be able to choose a method that they are most comfortable with and thus adhere to over the 10-week intervention and beyond.

The CBSM intervention is a group-based, closed structured, and sequenced intervention that meets once weekly for 2–2.5 hours over a 10-week period in groups of six to eight men facilitated by two group leaders. Chapter 2 provides more information on the logistics of running the group program. Using a group format allows us to (a) use group members and group leaders as coping role models where participants can make positive social comparisons and use social support for informational purposes; (b) encourage emotional expression and acceptance, and provide the opportunity to seek emotional and instrumental social support; (c) replace feelings of helplessness with a sense of mastery and altruism (e.g., self-efficacy changes); and (d) discourage avoidance and encourage acceptance, reframing, planning, problem-solving, and other adaptive coping strategies. Furthermore, participating in a group that is composed of other men who share a common experience and possibly similar challenges provides a sense of commonality that may offer an opportunity to access and benefit from various processes that would not be available in individual psychotherapy. Because our groups are led by two facilitators, the intervention occurs in a nurturing and safe environment where participants feel comfortable sharing private and sensitive processes while at the same time providing opportunities for support and challenges by other participants. This format provides an optimal atmosphere for encouraging emotional expression and an opportunity to seek and obtain emotional support from other group members in a safe and confidential environment.

Use of the Client Workbook

The *Cognitive-Behavioral Stress Management for Prostate Cancer Recovery, Workbook* provides group members with the necessary materials to participate in the program and will aid group leaders in delivering the intervention. Each workbook chapter corresponds to a session of the program and includes psychoeducational information about stress management techniques and basic instructions for relaxation exercises. The workbook provides participants with forms and worksheets for completing in-session activities that are designed to raise stress awareness and to practice applying stress management techniques to ongoing stressors. In addition to the in-session activities, each workbook session contains a take-home activity designed to help participants apply their newly acquired sets of CBSM techniques to both general and PCa-specific stressors. Participants complete monitoring forms each week and discuss their progress in learning and applying relaxation and stress management techniques during each weekly group meeting. Most monitoring forms can be photocopied from the workbook or downloaded from the Treatments *That Work*™ website at www.oup.com/us/ttw.

Together, the *Cognitive-Behavioral Stress Management for Prostate Cancer Recovery, Facilitator Guide* and *Workbook* make up the backbone of the CBSM program and should be used together in implementing the intervention with PCa survivors. Because the *Facilitator Guide* contains several "toggle" points where group leaders are instructed to incorporate actual workbook pages into the activities carried out in the group meeting, participants should be instructed to bring their workbooks to every session.

Chapter 2

Logistics of the Cognitive-Behavioral Stress Management Intervention Program

Group Meetings and Program Duration

Our Cognitive-Behavioral Stress Management (CBSM) program for prostate cancer survivors is designed to be implemented as a group-based psychosocial intervention that consists of 10 sessions delivered over a continuous 10-week period. The CBSM group sessions last 2–2.5 hours and are divided into two segments: a relaxation training component and a stress management component. During the first segment, participants are trained in conducting various relaxation exercises such as diaphragmatic breathing and progressive muscle relaxation (PMR). Following the relaxation training, participants are given a 15-minute break that is then followed by the stress management segment. This segment targets a specific stress management skill such as cognitive restructuring and coping skills training. We have used this format in all our CBSM interventions and it is well received by our participants. Conducting the relaxation training first allows participants to settle in, relax, and focus on the day's session, particularly if they are dealing with ongoing stressors.

It is important that the group facilitators and all participants agree on an optimal meeting time and location that works for everyone to maximize group attendance. Before the first session, group leaders should also ask participants about any prescheduled activities such as appointments or travel to plan ahead for any missed sessions. Because our CBSM sessions build on the content provided in the previous group meetings, it is critical that participants "keep up" and "stay in sequence" with other participants. At times it may be useful for a facilitator to schedule a "check in" call with a participant who missed a session to make sure he is keeping up in the workbook and to encourage attendance at the subsequent session.

Group Size

In our experience conducting CBSM groups we have learned that the optimal size of a CBSM group is between six to eight participants led by two group leaders or facilitators. This number ensures an adequate balance for participant disclosure, expression, and interactions, as well as group leader monitoring. Because our CBSM intervention involves having participants discuss their own experiences in a variety of topics, both cancer and non-cancer related, having more than eight participants may compromise the group's ability to process this information. Conversely, having fewer than three participants may prevent adequate discussion and application of the stress management skills, as the facilitators typically draw from participants' experiences to conduct group discussions and role-play dyads. While it is useful to have an even-numbered size group to conduct some of the exercises in the CBSM sessions, it is not necessary since a group leader can fill in to form a dyad with a participant in odd-numbered groups.

Closed Group Format

Our CBSM program is structured to deliver 10 weekly sessions that follow a sequence of relaxation and stress management techniques that progressively build on one another. Therefore, it is important that all participants acquire these skills in the specific order that they are delivered over the 10-week period. Because of this sequenced structure, it is vital that the CBSM program is delivered in a closed group format. In some instances, it is possible to allow a participant to join the CBSM program in the second or third weekly session. However, it is critical that the facilitator reviews the missed initial sessions with the participant, as many of the skills presented in the subsequent sessions build on the materials presented in sessions 1 and 2. Furthermore, session 1 covers important information such as group format and rules, confidentiality, and expectations, and it is very important that a participant joining at a later session has a clear understanding of this material.

The 10-week CBSM program follows a logical progression of skills presentation that begins with simple and straightforward techniques and advances to more complex combinations of different procedures. Because the CBSM intervention teaches many relaxation and stress management techniques over a relatively short period of time, deviating from the sequence of the 10 sessions will compromise participants' ability to fully comprehend and apply the techniques. Therefore, while it may be enticing to tailor the program to the specific needs of a particular group, it is essential that the facilitators stay "on track" within the session and over the 10-week period. For example, in the first session, we introduce PMR using eight muscle groups; session 2 combines diaphragmatic breathing with 4-muscle-group PMR; and session 3 incorporates a deep breathing and counting exercise with passive muscle relaxation. Over the course of the 10-week program, additional relaxation exercises are presented including imagery, two different types of meditation (mantra and mindfulness), and autogenic training. Many of these exercises are combined with diaphragmatic breathing; thus, this breathing exercise must be introduced before progressing to the other relaxation techniques.

Our stress management segment of CBSM follows a similar logical sequence of didactics. For example, our first session introduces participants to the concept of stress and awareness, which provides a foundation for better understanding the appraisal process introduced in session 2 and how emotions and thoughts are related. Session 3 builds on the prior two sessions to address how to break the cycle of negative thoughts and feelings, and so on. This sequence is based on a four-component theory that groups stress management techniques into (a) awareness-raising activities, (b) appraisal activities, (c) coping responses, and (d) use of coping resources. In addition to acquiring these basic stress management skills, our participants learn how these stress management processes are interrelated and how they can be used together in stressful situations. Therefore, our program begins with a simple understanding of stress awareness and progresses to a more complex set of steps that involves integrating information presented across the sessions. For example, the earlier sessions of CBSM focus on teaching participants cognitive strategies for monitoring how stress affects thoughts, feelings, and physical sensations; identifying inaccurate thoughts; and conducting a thorough appraisal of the stressors to determine whether they are controllable or uncontrollable. As the program progresses, participants learn behavioral techniques that facilitate engaging in adequate coping strategies that are matched to the nature of the stressor (controllable vs. uncontrollable). Toward the end of the program, the focus of the didactics is on learning interpersonal techniques, such as anger expression, assertiveness, and using social support, while incorporating previously learned cognitive and behavioral strategies.

Maintenance Sessions

Because our CBSM program is delivered over a relatively short period of time (10 weeks), at its completion we have used monthly maintenance sessions over a 6-month period to (a) reinforce the skills learned over the course of the intervention and (b) allow participants to draw from new and more recent experiences to apply their acquired CBSM skills. During the maintenance sessions, participants are encouraged to describe recent stressors they have experienced and the extent to which they have been able to employ the CBSM skills. In addition, participants identify barriers to engaging in CBSM techniques such as relaxation practice and how they have addressed these barriers. Over the course of the maintenance sessions, participants may have had an opportunity to adapt or develop alternative coping strategies, integrate a "favorite" relaxation skill into their regular schedules, or extend their social networks and practice of interpersonal skills. These are valuable experiences that can be shared with other group members to foster maintenance of learned skills and facilitate ongoing stress management.

On completion of the maintenance period, participants are offered the opportunity to continue to meet on a monthly basis with one of the group leaders in an open group format. We also refer participants to other ongoing support groups at local organizations for prostate cancer survivors. Affording participants the opportunity to continue to engage in maintenance sessions helps them continue to develop and enhance their stress management skills. It also provides participants with a supportive group environment where they can share their accomplishments, as well as frustrations and concerns over new and ongoing stressors in their lives.

Training Group Leaders

This CBSM manual is designed to be an appropriate guide for any health care professional (e.g., clinical psychologist, nurse, licensed clinical social worker) with previous group therapy and mental health training experience. In the development and delivery stages of our CBSM program, we used master's level ($<$ 2 years of clinical training) clinical health psychology graduate students and clinical psychology PhD level faculty to deliver the program. In some cases, it may be possible for non-mental health care professionals with extensive experience in conducting manualized patient support groups to implement the CBSM program with little difficulty. We do recommend, however, that all group facilitators complete a training sequence conducted over a 10-week period before facilitating the CBSM program, guided by the *Facilitator Guide* and supervised by a licensed mental health professional. Our facilitator training program has involved intensive in-class training in relaxation techniques such as PMR, guided imagery, diaphragmatic breathing, autogenics, and meditation. In addition, we conducted intensive training in the delivery of cognitive restructuring, coping skills training, anger management, and assertiveness training. Facilitators in training were also paired with experienced group leaders to conduct role playing exercises. Our training sessions were audiotaped and reviewed by licensed clinical supervisors to ensure proper adherence to protocol. In addition to this training, all our facilitators were assigned readings in relevant areas such as counseling issues with older adults with cancer, quality of life after prostate cancer, psychosocial aspects of sexual dysfunction, and the nature of the group therapy process and therapy with men.

In addition to extensive training protocols, all our CSBM groups were videotaped (with our participants' consent). Each session was reviewed by a clinical supervisor on a weekly basis. The videotapes were reviewed for treatment fidelity and used for weekly face-to-face supervision meetings with the facilitators. We have been successfully using these training and monitoring procedures over the past two decades in our various

CBSM programs (e.g., for people living with HIV/AIDS, breast cancer, and chronic fatigue syndrome), including those for men treated for prostate cancer. However, the clinicians using this program may want to use other systems that ensure the validity of the delivery of this intervention. The fidelity checklists included in an appendix may be used as part of the supervision process or to rate self-adherence. These forms may be photocopied from the book.

Relaxation Scripts and Use of Audio Recordings

The majority of the relaxation exercises used in this program are simplified versions of commonly used and validated relaxation exercises. The CBSM facilitators are encouraged to review full-length versions of several of these procedures in *The Relaxation and Stress Reduction Workbook* (Davis, Eshelman & McKay, 1988), *Hypnosis for Change, 3rd Ed.* (Hadley and Staudacher, 1996), the *Guide to Stress Reduction* (Mason, 1985), and *Full Catastrophe Living* (Kabat-Zinn, 1990).

Based on our experience in conducting relaxation training, we recommend that the facilitators make audio recordings of the relaxation script to be used by the participants at home. This approach facilitates effective adherence to relaxation practice and is particularly useful for the imagery exercises.

Chapter 3

Session 1: Introduction to the Program / Stress Awareness and Physical Responses / 8-Muscle-Group Progressive Muscle Relaxation

(Corresponds to overview chapter and session 1 of the workbook)

Materials Needed

- Diagram of prostate

- Flip chart or board

- Copy of participant workbook

- Comfortable chairs for relaxation training

- Copies of relaxation tapes (optional)

- Copies of monitoring sheets (optional)

- Copies of session evaluation sheet (optional)

Facilitator Note

- *This session runs longer than the other sessions. Allow extra time for the first meeting to introduce the program.*

INTRODUCTION TO THE PROGRAM

Outline

- Introduce co-leaders and provide positive reinforcement (5 minutes)

- Present general program information (15 minutes)

- Conduct reporter exercise (15 minutes)

- Describe structure of the program (10 minutes)

- Provide information about prostate cancer (25 minutes)

Introduction (5 minutes)

At the beginning of the first session, introduce yourselves as the group's co-leaders. Also, provide positive reinforcement of participants for coming to the group. Highlight the group members' shared experiences with prostate cancer; normalize similarities and differences.

General Program Information (15 minutes)

Tell the group that this program teaches stress management, coping strategies, and relaxation exercises to improve men's well-being as they cope with having had prostate cancer. The group will meet for 10 weeks, and every week new topics will be introduced. Stress that each module builds on the previous week; so it is important that group members attend all sessions. Explain that although there will be a didactic portion to each session, the real heart of every meeting is the input group members provide regarding their experiences and feelings, not only as they relate to their diagnoses or treatments, but in other areas of their lives that may have been affected by their diagnoses. You may want to use the following dialogue in your discussion:

> *Throughout the program, you will hear us refer to having prostate cancer, or having had prostate cancer. We do not mean to imply that you are ill, or that the cancer was not removed when you had surgery. When we speak of prostate cancer, we are not only referring to the tumor, but also to the entire life experience. In fact, you may be surprised to find that we will be talking much less about prostate cancer than you may have expected. In our view, we see the diagnosis of cancer as the starting point of a kind of crisis (a "growth crisis"). This crisis not only involves a change in your health status, but it often begins a series of changes in the way you see yourself, the way you see the*

world, your work and leisure activities, and your many relationships
with others. We see this time as an opportunity to help you have a
clearer picture of what you think, feel, and do about these changes.

Before continuing, field any questions or concerns from the group. Review the meeting time, place, and number of sessions for this particular group.

Confidentiality

One concern throughout this program is preserving the safety for each group member to speak openly and candidly about his experiences. Emphasize that confidentiality is an important condition of the group process. Explain that some of the group members may know each other from before, or may have friends in common, or may go to the same doctor. Many of them may live in the same area or frequent the same places and thus may run into each other outside the group. It is very important for everyone to keep very strict confidentiality about what is said in group so members can speak naturally. The following dialogue may be helpful:

> *When speaking with others outside the group, you can feel free to talk*
> *about what you experienced, what you learned, or what you felt in the*
> *group, but please don't talk about other people's experiences, even*
> *without using their names. You see, that often does not end up being*
> *confidential. If others know someone is in the group, and they hear*
> *about "so-and-so," sometimes they can guess from the context who it is,*
> *and there goes the group's confidentiality.*

Inquire if the group has any questions and if everyone can agree to adhere to the rules of confidentiality.

Learning from Other's Experiences

Discuss the limitations of co-leaders and highlight the contributions of group members with the following dialogue:

As group leaders, we bring our knowledge and experiences to the group. However, we also know that many of you have already done a lot of work to increase your awareness of prostate cancer. While we can provide you with some tools to deal with stress, we have not experienced what it is like to have prostate cancer firsthand. And because we have not been through your experiences, we do not claim to know exactly what this has been like for you. Much of your learning will be from sharing your experiences and listening to the experiences of other members of the group.

Emphasize that everyone experiences difficult life events, and subsequently learns and grows from them; this is why it is so beneficial to participate in a group setting such as this.

Expectations of Program

Tell the group that you would like to hear from each of them about any other expectations they might have of you, of the program, and of themselves.

Reporter Exercise (15 minutes)

Next, take some time to let group members get to know each other. It can be helpful to begin with the "reporter exercise." Instructions for this exercise are included in session 1 of the participant workbook.

Have the group break up into pairs and members interview one another. After pairs have talked for a few minutes, each person will report back to the group about what he has learned about his partner. In his report, each person should include an adjective (e.g., funny, smart, athletic) that describes his partner, as well as what his partner expects to gain from participating in this group.

Or, alternatively, have group members introduce themselves, give their general life information, and state any particular concerns or expectations they have regarding this group. If a group member either neglects to mention information about his diagnosis or only discusses his diagnosis, encourage him to broaden his introduction.

Structure of the Program (10 minutes)

Explain that each weekly meeting will have two parts: learning about stress management and relaxation training. The group will focus on ways to deal with stress in a healthy and effective manner. Participants will learn how to use these skills in stressful situations they encounter in their daily lives—at work, at home, or in social situations. Emphasize that most people experience some type of stressful situation every so often, and some more than others.

Stress Management

The stress management component involves group discussion about stressful situations that participants may encounter, everyday situations that group members may bring up, issues related to prostate cancer, etc. Each session will introduce some new information and will usually include an exercise to be completed. Some participants may feel uncomfortable or anxious when certain topics are discussed. At times they may even prefer not to talk about certain things. Emphasize, however, that it is very important that they attend every session, and that the group discusses certain topics and concerns. If any group members are anxious or uncomfortable with a topic, you will work with them to learn how to handle those emotions, so that they can benefit from the information the group is providing. At this point, ask for examples of topics that might be less comfortable to talk about. If no one volunteers any examples, suggest problems with sexual intimacy (e.g., ED, sexual dysfunction), incontinence, anger, or disruptions in relationships with a spouse, partner, or family member.

Explain that each meeting covers different topics. This week, session 1, covers information about prostate cancer and how to become aware of stress and its physical effects. Following weeks will include topics such as stress awareness and appraisal, sexuality and sex after prostate cancer treatment, cognitive distortions, cognitive restructuring, coping strategies, anger management, assertiveness, and social support.

Next inform group members that the didactic and discussion portion of each week will include:

- learning new information

- participating in exercises that help process the information

- sharing experiences with the group

- receiving weekly homework assignments

Emphasize that the stress management component will require practice on each participant's part outside the sessions. There will be assignments every week using the participant workbook. It is very important that members do them to get the most benefit from the program. Use the following dialogue to highlight the importance of homework:

> We will need your commitment on doing homework. These will be very practical assignments, like paying attention to how stressed you are, the things you say to yourself, and how you feel when you are stressed. Most people find these exercises both interesting and useful. Remember that the weekly assignments are just as important as the group meetings. In a way, completing these weekly assignments helps you put to work the skills learned in group in day-to-day situations.

Relaxation Training

The second component of each session is relaxation training. These exercises address the physiological, cognitive, and emotional aspects of stress. This part consists of learning:

- techniques that address physical tension

- techniques that provide relief from ruminating and recurrent negative thoughts

- self-suggestion to help relax oneself at will

It is very important for group members to practice relaxation exercises outside the sessions to benefit from them. Findings of the authors' study suggest that the participants who got the most benefit from groups were those who felt confident about their ability to engage in relaxation techniques when faced with stressful situations (Penedo, et al., 2006). The following dialogue can be used to emphasize home practice:

> *Daily practice on your own is the only way that you will get full benefit of using the techniques. We will ask you to practice the relaxation exercises every day for the full 10 weeks of the program. Most people find it enjoyable to take this time to relax every day, but sometimes people have a hard time fitting it into their schedules. Together we will discuss strategies for incorporating relaxation exercises into your daily routine.*

To help them identify times when they can incorporate relaxation into their daily routines, group members will be completing the Activity Log in the workbook as part of the homework.

Prostate Cancer Information (25 minutes)

Begin today's didactic portion with a brief discussion of what the prostate is, prostate cancer in general, and the common side effects that many men experience. Say that you know that many participants may have done some research prior to their surgeries, so they should feel free to add to your information.

The Prostate

Use overheads, a model, and/or poster of a prostate to illustrate function and changes after removal (see Figure 3.1). Or refer group members to the copy of the diagram in the participant workbook. This section includes some basic information about the prostate to share with the group.

The prostate is a walnut-shaped gland located just below the bladder and just in front of the rectum. Because of where it is situated, the doctor

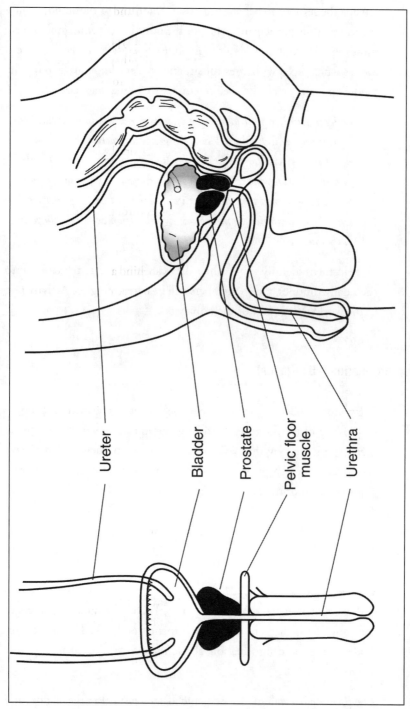

Male urinary tract, front and side views.

Figure 3.1

Diagram of a Prostate

Source: US Department of Health and Human Services, NIH Publication No. 07-5105, October 2006

Ureter

Bladder

Prostate

Pelvic floor muscle

Urethra

can feel the contour of the prostate when he or she performs a rectal examination. A normal prostate gland is smooth and firm, but not hard.

The prostate is made up of many different cell types that have complex and poorly understood interactions with each other. The male hormone testosterone and its related hormones have major roles in the growth and function of the prostate.

The prostate plays an essential function in human reproduction. The prostate secretes fluids and enzymes that make up about one-third of the spermatic fluid that leaves the body during ejaculation. The sperm in the ejaculate is made in the testicles and transported through a tube called the vas deferens. This tube also passes through and receives additional fluids from the prostate before reaching the urethra. The urethra is the tube inside the penis through which urine and ejaculate pass. The seminal vesicles are structures that lie right behind and slightly above the prostate and secrete fluids, which are added to the ejaculate.

Prostate Cancer

Prostate cancer is a *malignancy*, or a bunch of cancerous cells that grow very rapidly. It develops in the prostate gland, an important organ for the proper function of the male reproductive system. A cancer diagnosis includes the "stage" of the disease. Some people misunderstand this to mean that the cancer progresses through stages, starting with Stage I. Rather, the stage of cancer refers to the *size* of the tumor when it is detected, and whether the cancer has *spread* to surrounding tissues, lymph nodes, or other parts of the body. Stage I or II is called "early stage" disease; in these stages the cancer is only inside the prostate gland.

According to the American Cancer Society (www.cancer.org, 2006), one in six men will be affected by prostate cancer, making it the most common cancer among American men other than skin cancer. For men with Stage I or II cancer (localized prostate cancer), there is almost a 100% chance that they will be alive five years from diagnosis.

PSA Test

PSA is an abbreviation for prostate-specific antigen, which is a protein made by the glandular cells of the prostate. A small amount continuously leaks into the blood. The amount circulating in the blood can be measured by a blood test. The amount of PSA in the blood can increase with certain abnormal conditions which affect the prostate gland, such as infection, benign enlargement of the prostate, and cancer of the prostate. Although recurrence of prostate cancer that is treated at an early stage is not common, men undergo ongoing monitoring of their PSA levels to make sure there is no sign of the cancer coming back.

Who Gets Prostate Cancer?

Explain that we do not yet know the cause of prostate cancer; however, we do know some factors that increase the risk of getting prostate cancer. (Adapted from www.drkoop.com, 2000.)

Family History: Having a father or brother with prostate cancer doubles a man's chances of developing the disease.

Age: The risk is greater for older men. Three-quarters of all reported cases occur in men age 65 and older.

Ethnicity/Race: African-American and black men in the U.S. have the highest incidence of prostate cancer in the world, are two times more likely to be diagnosed with the disease, and two-and-a-half to three times more likely to die of prostate cancer.

Hormone Levels: Since eunuchs (men who have been castrated) do not get the disease, this suggests that the male hormones produced by the testicles influence the development of prostate cancer. Also, high levels of testosterone (a male hormone) have been associated with development and progression of prostate cancer.

Environmental Factors: The rate of prostate cancer for members of the same racial group varies by where they live, suggesting that differences in environment or diet may have an effect, though this remains to be proven. For example, the Asian population has a low risk of prostate cancer; but when Asian men immigrate to the United States, their incidence of prostate cancer increases.

Types and Side Effects of Treatment for Prostate Cancer

There are several types of treatment available for prostate cancer. These are:

- Surgery (prostatectomy)

- Radiation therapy

- Hormonal therapy

- Chemotherapy

The two main side effects of radical prostatectomy are incontinence and impotence. Review key facts for each side effect.

Incontinence

Incontinence is the inability to control the urine stream, resulting in leakage or dribbling of urine. Normal bladder control usually returns within several weeks or months after radical prostatectomy.

Passing a small amount of urine when coughing, laughing, sneezing, or exercising is known as stress incontinence. This may persist permanently after prostatectomy in up to 35% of men. Some patients (between 2% and 5%) have more serious stress incontinence, which may be permanent (Peyromaure, Ravery, & Boccon-Gibod, 2002).

Impotence

Impotence, also known as erectile dysfunction or ED, is an inability to get an erection of the penis.

The nerves that allow men to get erections may be damaged or removed by radical prostatectomy. The effect of this operation on a man's ability to achieve an erection is related to the patient's age and whether nerve-sparing surgery was done. Nearly all men who have a radical prostatectomy should expect some permanent decrease in their ability to have an erection, but younger men may expect to retain more of their ability.

During the first three to 12 months after radical prostatectomy, most men will have erectile dysfunction and will need to use medications or other treatments if they want to have an erection. Several solutions for impotence are available:

- Prostheses (penile implants)

- Prostaglandin E1 injections (a substance naturally produced in the body that can produce erections)

- Vacuum devices

- Viagra® (sildenafil citrate)

- Cialis® (tadalafil)

Mention that the group will spend some time discussing issues related to sex and sexuality in later sessions.

Life After Treatment

Tell participants that although the statistics for men with prostate cancer are promising, there are additional things they can do to regain a sense of control and feel healthy. In fact, they are doing one of them right now by being here to learn how to manage their stress. Emphasize that changing unhealthy lifestyle behaviors may be an extremely important factor in preventing recurrence of cancer (Amling et. al, 2004). Recurrence, although not common, is a real possibility, even after a successful surgery. Make sure that everyone in the group understands that it is important to get regular medical check-ups with a urologist and regular PSA tests. Inquire if there are any questions or comments before continuing with the stress management section.

Outline

- Define stress (5 minutes)

- Describe the effects of stress (10 minutes)

- Have group members complete the symptoms of stress checklist (5 minutes)

- Discuss the physical effects of stress (10 minutes)

- Review the link between stress and cancer (5 minutes)

- Discuss optional topics (5 minutes)

- Assign homework (5 minutes)

Definition of Stress (5 minutes)

Define stress as when an event leads to physical, mental, or emotional tension. When we are feeling this tension we say we are feeling "stressed out." It is possible to distinguish between "stress" and "a stressor." Stress is the response we feel in our bodies. However, a stressor is the actual event or situation that we interpret as stressful or challenging. Discuss with group members how they define stress.

Effects of Stress (10 minutes)

Explain to the group that sometimes we are not even aware that we are experiencing stress. Becoming familiar with the physical cues that indicate we are feeling stressed is often the first step in increasing our awareness of our responses to stress. Sometimes, when we recognize these responses, we can tell we are feeling stressed and can then work backward to identify the source of this stress (i.e., the stressor). Also, our knowledge and awareness can help us in using the appropriate technique for our individual symptoms. Most of the effects of stress fall into five categories:

Cognitive (our thoughts): anxious thoughts, fearful anticipation, poor concentration, difficulty with memory

Emotional (our feelings): feelings of tension, worry, irritability, restlessness, inability to relax, depression

Behavioral (how we act): avoidance of tasks, sleep problems, difficulty in completing work assignments, fidgeting, crying, changes in drinking, eating, or smoking behaviors

Physical (what we feel in our bodies): stiff or tense muscles, teeth grinding, clenched fists, sweating, tension headaches, feeling faint, choking feeling, difficulty swallowing, stomach ache, loss of interest in sex, tiredness, awareness of heart beating

Social (how we act toward others): avoiding others, isolating ourselves, seeking out other people, venting, getting easily irritated with others

Symptoms of Stress Checklist (5 minutes)

Have group members fill out the Symptoms of Stress Checklist found in the workbook. Draw a 5-box grid on the board and fill it in according to participants' responses (Table 3.1)

Discuss the stress responses of participants and the cues that indicate they are experiencing stress.

Table 3.1 Sample Grid Listing Participants' Responses to Symptoms of Stress

Cognitive/ Thoughts	Emotional/ Feelings	Behavioral/ Actions	Physical/Body Sensations	Social/ Relationships
Distracted "I'm not a real man anymore."	Angry Depressed	Overeating Procrastinating Not sleeping well	Headaches Muscle tension Tiredness	Withdrawing Short with others

Physical Effects of Stress (10 minutes)

Reinforce that we need stress management because stress affects us mentally, emotionally, behaviorally, physically, and socially. This section focuses on the physical effects of stress. Introduce the concept of the "fight-or-flight" response to the group. The following paragraphs include information to include in your discussion.

The effects of the "fight-or-flight" response enable the person to take quick action in response to the stressor. Use the following dialogue to illustrate:

> *For example, if you were swimming in the ocean and noticed a shark swimming nearby, you would want to get out of the water pretty quickly. That is the "flight" part. However, if someone attacks you physically, you would need additional strength to fight them, hence the "fight" part.*

Common physical effects associated with the "fight-or-flight" response include:

■ pupils dilate

■ respiration increases

■ heart rate increases

■ blood pressure increases

■ blood flows to muscles, away from organs

■ sweat glands are stimulated

■ sugar and fatty acids are released into the blood

■ adrenal gland releases adrenaline and noradrenaline

In our society, physical action is rarely the best way to deal with the stress we encounter. For example, when the boss is making excessive demands, it's best not to punch him. Our body still responds physically, even though we are not dealing with the stress in a physically active manner. However, the "fight-or-flight" response was adaptive for our ancestors. It helped them get out of the way or defend themselves when an animal (like a saber-toothed tiger) was hungry for lunch.

Though designed to help protect us from danger, this physiological reaction can be harmful to our bodies. It takes its toll if it is repeated on a regular basis. It may be associated with poorer recovery from illness, an exacerbation of symptoms of chronic diseases, and impairment of cardiac and immune functioning (Segerstrom & Miller, 2004).

Link Between Stress and Cancer (5 minutes)

Group members may wonder if stress caused their cancer. The answer is probably not. As discussed previously, cancer is caused by many different factors. Research suggests that genetics, environment, diet, stress, and other factors may play a role in the development of cancer (American Cancer Society, 2007). Remind participants that blaming oneself for getting cancer is not a productive exercise. We have learned, however, that stress can make an already-existing condition worse and can reduce a person's quality of life (Luecken & Compas, 2002).

Use the following diagram to illustrate the effect stress can have on cancer progression. Inform the group that although stress does not directly cause cancer, we know that when someone is experiencing stress, he is more likely to engage in unhealthy habits (e.g., eating a poor diet, smoking, not sleeping well, drinking too much alcohol). All these activities can increase the risk of cancer (American Cancer Society, 2007). Also, stress is known to directly affect the immune system; for example, we are more likely to get a cold when under stress (Cohen, Doyle, & Skoner,

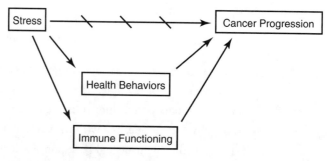

Figure 3.2
Diagram of the Effect of Stress on Cancer Progression

1999). Explain that the reason for this relationship is that when we are stressed out, our bodies produce stress hormones that can affect how well our immune systems work. This program will help participants reduce stress to maximize immune system functioning and possibly improve overall physical health.

Optional Discussion Topics (5 minutes)

If time allows, discuss how group members perceive the mind–body relationship. Ask the group members if they have heard of the mind–body connection. Refer to the link between stress and a cold, and stress and cancer. We now know that the mind—that is, how we think and feel emotionally—can have physiological effects on the body. Emphasize that the mind and body are not independent of one another. This program will teach participants how to improve how they process information around them. By improving their thinking or interpretation of events around them, their moods can be improved and eventually they may even begin to feel physically better.

You may also want to talk further about how prostate cancer is a multi-factorial disease—affected by so many factors such as lifestyle (diet, exercise, smoking), genetics, and other unknown factors. Stress that while we cannot always pinpoint the cause of the disease, there are things we can do to lessen the chance of recurrence. Some common sense practices include adequate medical follow-up as recommended by our doctor, eating better, getting enough sleep, engaging in physical activity according to our physician's recommendations, avoiding unhealthy habits such as smoking and heavy drinking, and of course, managing stress in an effective way.

Homework (5 minutes)

✎ Have group members review the overview chapter and session 1 of the workbook.

✎ Have group members complete the Stressful Events Worksheet.

✎ Have group members review the Symptoms of Stress Checklist.

Outline

■ Introduce progressive muscle relaxation and give rationale (10 minutes)

■ Review procedure and muscle groups for progressive muscle relaxation (10 minutes)

■ Conduct 8-Muscle-Group Progressive Muscle Relaxation (20 minutes)

■ Discuss relaxation experience and today's session (5 minutes)

■ Assign homework (5 minutes)

■ Have group members complete session evaluation sheet (5 minutes)

Progressive Muscle Relaxation Rationale and Introduction (10 minutes)

Remind participants that in the relaxation portion of the session they will be learning skills to help them manage the stress they encounter in their daily lives. Today, they will be taught a method of reducing physical tension by tensing and then releasing various muscle groups throughout the body. This process is called progressive muscle relaxation training or PMR.

Use the following information to provide background about PMR. Progressive muscle relaxation was first developed in the 1930s as people explored how tensing of muscles can be related to other physiological changes in the body. At the same time that muscles tense, hormones and other chemicals are released into the body. All of these responses are part of what prepares the body for "fight or flight." As discussed previously, repeated activation of the fight-or-flight response can have harmful effects on the body. One way to protect oneself is to learn how to turn off this response by producing relaxation in the muscles, which relieves tension in the body.

Inform the group that PMR training basically involves learning to tense and then relax various groups of muscles all through the body. While doing this, participants will be paying attention to the feelings associated with both tension and relaxation. Explain that first tensing the muscles helps achieve relaxation by creating momentum when the tension is released (like a pendulum swinging). It also accentuates the difference between tension and relaxation and helps us recognize when we are tense as opposed to relaxed.

Take a few minutes and ask group members about previous experiences with relaxation techniques.

Review of PMR Procedure and Muscle Groups (10 minutes)

Before beginning the PMR exercise, review the procedure and muscle groups to be used. Explain that participants will be breaking down muscles into eight groups and tensing and relaxing each group twice. After each relaxation, there will be some silent time to enjoy the feeling of relaxation. Also, at the end of the exercise, you will be quiet for 2–3 minutes before giving them instructions to come out of relaxation.

Demonstrate the muscles to be used. (See the 8-Muscle-Group script in the next section; instructions for each muscle group are also included in the workbook.)

Make an important point that participants should be careful not to tense too hard. They should not feel any pain or discomfort. If at any point they feel pain or cramping, they should release their muscles immediately and tense less the following time.

Also, point out that often, participants won't feel completely relaxed the first time they do this exercise. Like most things, it takes practice and the more they do the exercise, the easier it will be for them to relax.

Tell participants that if during the exercise they feel the need to cough or anything like that, not to hold back. They can feel free to leave quietly and get a drink of water, or do whatever they need to feel more comfortable. While one co-leader will lead the relaxation, the other will be available, so if they need anything they can signal him.

Last, stress that it is important for participants to try not to fall asleep. They need to be aware of what the relaxation exercise is like, and mindful of their relaxation response. If they do fall asleep, or if they don't wake up when the exercises are done or if they snore during the exercise, you'll just tap them lightly on the shoulder or foot.

8-Muscle-Group Progressive Muscle Relaxation (20 minutes)

One group leader presents PMR instructions while the other leader monitors relaxation levels of group members. Pause lengths in seconds are indicated in parentheses in the script. Each muscle group should be practiced twice in a row.

Arms Muscle Group

Build up the tension in your arms by making fists and holding your arms out in front of you with your elbows at a 45-degree angle. Notice the sensations of pulling, discomfort, and tightness in your hands, lower arms, and upper arms. Hold the tension. [Pause 10 seconds.] *Now release the tension and let your arms and hands relax, with palms facing down. Focus your attention on the sensations of relaxation through your hands, lower arms, and upper arms. As you relax, breathe smoothly and slowly from your abdomen. Each time you exhale, think the word "relax."* [Pause 20 seconds then repeat the muscle group for a second practice.]

Legs Muscle Group

Now, build up the tension in your legs by lifting your legs slightly off the floor and, if you feel comfortable, pointing your feet inward. Feel the tension as it moves up your feet into your ankles, shins, calves, and thighs. Feel the pulling sensations from the hip down. Hold the ten-

sion. [Pause 10 seconds.] *Now, release the tension, lowering your legs and relaxing the feet. Feel the warmth and heaviness of relaxation through your feet, lower legs, and upper legs. As you breathe smoothly and slowly, think the word "relax" each time you exhale.* [Pause 20 seconds then repeat the muscle group for a second practice.]

Stomach Muscle Group

Now, make your stomach hard by pulling your stomach in toward your spine very tightly. Feel the tightness of your stomach muscles. Focus on that part of your body and hold the tension. [Pause 10 seconds.] *Now, let your stomach relax outward. Let it go further and further. Feel the sense of warmth circulating across your stomach. Feel the soft comfort of relaxation. As you breathe smoothly and slowly, think the word "relax" each time you exhale.* [Pause 20 seconds then repeat the muscle group for a second practice.]

Chest Muscle Group

Now, build up the tension around your chest by taking a deep breath and holding it. Your chest is expanded, and the muscles are stretched around it. Feel the tension in your chest and back. Hold your breath. [Pause 10 seconds.] *Now, slowly, let the air escape and breathe normally, letting the air flow in and out smoothly and easily. Feel the difference as the muscles relax compared with the tension, and think the word "relax" each time you exhale.* [Pause 20 seconds then repeat the muscle group for a second practice.]

Shoulders and Upper Back Muscle Group

Pull your shoulder blades back and together. Feel the tension around your shoulders and radiating down into your back. Concentrate on the sensation of tension in this part of your body. [Pause 10 seconds.] *Now relax your shoulder blades and let them return to a normal position. Focus on the sense of relaxation around your shoulders and across your upper back. Feel the difference in these muscles from the tension. As you breathe smoothly and slowly, think the word "relax" each time you exhale.* [Pause 20 seconds then repeat the muscle group for a second practice.]

Neck Muscle Group

Build up the tension around your neck by pulling your chin down toward your chest and raising and tightening your shoulders. Feel the tightness around the back of your neck spreading up into the back of your head. Focus on the tension. [Pause 10 seconds.] *Now, release the tension, letting your head rest comfortably and your shoulders droop. Concentrate on the relaxation. Feel the difference from the tension. As you breathe smoothly and slowly, think the word "relax" each time you exhale.* [Pause 20 seconds then repeat the muscle group for a second practice.]

Mouth, Jaw, and Throat Muscle Group

Build up the tension around your mouth, jaw, and throat by clenching your teeth and forcing the corners of your mouth back into a forced smile. Feel the tightness, and concentrate on the sensations of tension. [Pause 10 seconds.] *Then, release the tension, letting your mouth drop open and the muscles around your throat and jaw relax. Concentrate on the difference in the sensations in that part of your body. As you breathe smoothly and slowly, think the word "relax" each time you exhale.* [Pause 20 seconds then repeat the muscle group for a second practice.]

Eyes and Forehead Muscle Group

Squeeze your eyes tightly shut while pulling your eyebrows down and toward the center. Feel the tension across your lower forehead and around the eyes. Concentrate on the tension. [Pause 10 seconds.] *Now release, letting the tension around your eyes slide away. Relax the forehead, smoothing out the wrinkles. Feel the difference of relaxation in comparison to tension. As you breathe smoothly and slowly, think the word "relax" each time you exhale.* [Pause 20 seconds then repeat the muscle group for a second practice.]

Whole Body Relaxation

Now your whole body is feeling relaxed and comfortable. As you feel yourself becoming even more relaxed, count from 1 to 5. One, letting all of the tension leave your body. Two, sinking further and further into relaxation. Three, feeling more and more relaxed. Four, feeling very relaxed. Five, feeling deeply relaxed. As you spend a few minutes in this relaxed state, think about your breathing. Feel the cool air as you breathe in and the warm air as you breathe out. Your breathing is slow and regular. Each time you breathe out, think the word "relax." (Pause 2 minutes). *Now, count backward from 5, gradually feeling yourself become more alert and awake. Five, feeling more awake. Four, coming out of relaxation. Three, feeling more alert. Two, opening your eyes. One, sitting up.*

Post-Relaxation Discussion (5 minutes)

Check in with group members to process their experience with Progressive Muscle Relaxation. Use the following questions:

- "What did you like?"

- "What didn't you like?"

- "What aspects were hard/easy for you?"

- "Can you practice this at home with the instructions in the workbook?"

If time allows, check in with participants about their overall experience in the group today.

- "Any questions about today's session?"

- "Any comments/opinions about today's session?"

Homework (5 minutes)

✎ Have group members complete the Activity Log in the workbook and find time for relaxation in their schedules.

✎ Have group members practice 8-Muscle-Group PMR at least once a day. They should record stress levels before and after each practice on the Relaxation Monitoring Sheet.

✎ Remind participants about stress management homework. Have them repeat the instructions to make sure they understand what they are being asked to do. Reinforce the importance of homework, and of practicing relaxation at home.

Facilitator Note

■ *Basic instructions for all relaxation exercises are included in the workbook. It is recommended that you provide group members with copies of audio recordings of the scripts used in session. Group members will also be using the Relaxation Monitoring Sheet every week; a copy is provided in each session of the workbook. If you would like to provide additional copies for the group, you may photocopy this sheet from the workbook.* ■

Session Evaluation (5 minutes) (optional)

Have group members complete the session evaluation sheet (see appendix).

| **Chapter 4** | *Session 2: Diaphragmatic Breathing and 4-Muscle-Group Progressive Muscle Relaxation / Stress Awareness and the Appraisal Process* |

(Corresponds to session 2 of the workbook)

Materials Needed

- PMR script from session 1

- Flip chart or board

- Copy of participant workbook

- Comfortable chairs for relaxation training

- Copies of relaxation tapes (optional)

- Copies of monitoring sheets (optional)

- Copies of session evaluation sheet (optional)

RELAXATION TRAINING: *Diaphragmatic Breathing and 4-Muscle-Group Progressive Muscle Relaxation*

Outline

- Discuss adherence to relaxation practice (5 minutes)

- Introduce diaphragmatic breathing and give rationale (5 minutes)

- Conduct diaphragmatic breathing exercise (10 minutes)

- Conduct progressive muscle relaxation for four muscle groups (15 minutes)

- Discuss relaxation practice (3 minutes)

- Assign homework (2 minutes)

Discussion of Adherence to Relaxation Practice (5 minutes)

Talk about things that facilitate doing exercises at home or at work as well as problems that group members are encountering with relaxation. Ask participants the following questions:

- "How often do you find you are able to practice the relaxation exercise?"

- "Where are you practicing relaxation?"

- "What gets in the way for you?"

Discuss use of the Relaxation Monitoring Sheet. Was it easy, difficult? What were the barriers to use? Problem-solve ways that the men can practice relaxation techniques at home, and find ways they can remind themselves to use the sheet.

Optional: collect Relaxation Monitoring Sheets and distribute relaxation tapes.

Diaphragmatic Breathing Introduction and Rationale (5 minutes)

Tell participants that in today's session they will be learning one of the most practical and versatile forms of relaxation—the deep breathing exercise, or diaphragmatic breathing. Explain that proper breathing is important for stress management; it helps prepare the ground for the execution of more efficient coping strategies. When a person is relaxed and in good physical form, he starts out in the best possible position to respond to stressors. You may want to use the following information about breathing in your presentation.

When the body inhales, air is drawn in through the nose and warmed by the mucous membrane of the nasal passages. The bristly hairs of the nostrils filter out impurities, which are expelled on the next exhalation.

The diaphragm is a sheet-like muscle that stretches across the chest, separating the chest from the abdomen. Although one can voluntarily expand and contract the diaphragm, it operates largely automatically. When the diaphragm relaxes, the lungs contract and air is forced out. Diaphragmatic breaths are deep breaths that cause the abdomen to rise and fall.

Breathing naturally purifies and relaxes the body. The body is like a stress management machine, and oxygen is like gas for the cells. Blood travels from the heart to the lungs, where it is purified and oxygenated, and then returns to the left side of the heart and is pumped back out into the body.

When we become stressed, the tendency is to breathe less from the diaphragm and much more shallowly in the upper sections of the lungs. When an insufficient amount of fresh air reaches the lungs, the blood is not properly purified or oxygenated. How is this insufficiency related to one's health status? Digestion can be hampered. Organs and tissues may become undernourished and deteriorate. Poorly oxygenated blood may make a person more vulnerable to anxiety, depression, and fatigue, making stressful situations that much harder to cope with.

Importance of Practice

Tell participants that you are going to help them learn to use their diaphragms more efficiently to maximize the benefits of breathing. Breathing exercises have been found to be effective in reducing anxiety, depression, irritability, muscular tension, and fatigue (McCaul et al., 1979; Miller, 1987). While breathing exercises can be learned in minutes and can be done anywhere and anytime, the deeper effects of the exercise may not be fully appreciated until after months of persistent practice.

Emphasize that it will be important for participants to find a way to practice diaphragmatic breathing in their daily lives. At first, they may want to practice when they are relaxed and will not be disturbed. Once they become more skilled, however, they can begin to practice at other places and times during the day. They can practice diaphragmatic breathing in 30-second to 2-minute intervals, for example, while waiting for a red light or an elevator, or for someone to answer the phone. Since they have to breathe anyway, no one will know they are practicing breathing for relaxation. Remind participants that using diapghragmatic breathing during times of stress will help them relax and put them in a better position to respond to the situation.

Diaphragmatic Breathing Exercise (10 minutes)

Briefly demonstrate the basics of deep breathing. Use the following instructions to take the group through the exercise.

Get into a comfortable position. First check how you normally breathe by putting one hand on your stomach and the other hand on your chest. Inhale slowly and see which hand moves. Shallow breaths move the hand on the chest; diaphragmatic breaths move the hand on the stomach.

Now, practice taking diaphragmatic breaths. Slowly inhale through your nose. As you breathe in, feel your stomach expand with your hand. Exhale slowly out your mouth. As you breathe out, feel your stomach contract and sink in. Continue breathing deeply, noticing how your abdomen rises and falls with each breath. With every breath, feel yourself becoming more and more relaxed.

4-Muscle-Group Progressive Muscle Relaxation (15 minutes)

Review the procedure and general instructions for PMR practice as outlined in session 1. Introduce the four muscle groups to be used and review the instructions for each group. Demonstrate the muscles to tense. Tell participants that they will tense and relax each group of muscles twice, and after each time, they will have some silent time to enjoy the feeling of relaxation.

Have participants begin with diaphragmatic breathing. Lead the group through progressive muscle relaxation for four muscle groups using the script from session 1 with the following adaptations:

1. *Arms:* Repeat instructions for this muscle group

2. *Legs:* Repeat instructions for this muscle group

3. *Stomach, Chest, Shoulders and Upper Back:* Combine instructions for these muscle groups

4. *Neck, Mouth, Jaw, and Throat:* Combine instructions for these muscle groups.

You may want to end the exercise with the script for whole body relaxation (see session 1).

Post-Relaxation Discussion Questions (3 minutes)

- "What did you like?"

- "What didn't you like?"

- "What aspects were hard/easy for you?"

- "Can you practice this at home using the instructions in the workbook?"

Homework (2 minutes)

✎ Have group members practice diaphragmatic breathing at least once a day. They should record stress levels before and after each practice on the Relaxation Monitoring Sheet.

✎ Have group members practice 4-Muscle-Group PMR at least once a day. They should record stress levels before and after each practice on the Relaxation Monitoring Sheet.

STRESS MANAGEMENT: *Stress Awareness and the Appraisal Process*

Outline

- Check in with group members (5 minutes)

- Review material and homework from the previous session (5 minutes)

- Discuss the importance of awareness to stress management (5 minutes)

- Review the negative effects of stress (5 minutes)

- Create awareness of physical tension and sensations (20 minutes)

- Introduce the appraisal process (10 minutes)

- Discuss the connection between appraisals, emotions, and reactions (10 minutes)

- Practice the appraisal process (10 minutes)

- Assign homework (5 minutes)

- Have group members complete session evaluation sheet (5 minutes) (optional)

Pre-Didactic Check-In (5 minutes)

Go around the room and have each group member share how he is doing and update other group members on any personal news.

Previous Material and Homework Review (5 minutes)

Briefly review the main points from last session's stress management section. Answer any questions group members may have. Note that members may hesitate to ask questions from the earlier sessions. Use prompts such as:

> *This material is new to most of you and at times can be a bit of a challenge to understand or relate to your daily lives. Now is a good time to ask any questions you may have.*

Review assigned stress management homework (e.g., Stressful Events Worksheet). Problem-solve any difficulties group members had completing the homework.

Importance of Awareness to Stress Management (5 minutes)

Stress management consists of strategies that help us become more *aware* of situations that cause stress and it aims to provide more effective techniques for coping with stress. Explain to participants that one goal of this stress management intervention is to help them become more aware of:

- The situations in which they are most likely to experience stress—these may be directly related to medical issues (e.g., unable to achieve erection, having difficulty dealing with their medical team), indirectly related (e.g., needing to urinate but being stuck in traffic), or unrelated (e.g., feeling angry with a friend for not returning some tools he borrowed)

- Their typical reaction to stressful events (e.g., cursing, yelling, seeking revenge, holding it in)

- How their thoughts regarding these situations are related to how they feel emotionally

- Ways in which these cognitive-emotional events shape their behavior and their sense of confidence and self-esteem

Negative Effects of Stress (Stress Isn't Good for You) (5 minutes)

When an event is interpreted as stressful, it sets off a complex physiological response that involves the body's glands and organs. Review the following effects the fight-or-flight response has on the body:

1. In response to the need for action, heart rate and respiration speed up and increased amounts of sugar and fatty acids are released into the body.

2. In anticipation of bodily damage, hormones (corticosteroids) are released. The effects of these hormones are to reduce fever, reduce inflammation, and increase the amount of energy available to the individual.

3. In anticipation of pain from injury or exertion, the body releases endogenous opiates. These act as pain relievers that enable the individual to continue to defend himself if injured or keep running away without having to stop. Endogenous opiates can give a sensation of well-being, for example, a "runner's high."

As previously mentioned, the fight-or-flight response made a lot of sense for our cavemen ancestors, as the stressors they faced were primarily physical stressors, such as encountering a saber-toothed tiger. Remind group members that today we tend to deal with stressors primarily in a passive manner. (Repeat the example of how it is generally not in one's best interest to punch one's boss when he is making excessive demands.) The body, however, still responds as if fight or flight is the only viable option. The physiological changes still take place and can have lasting negative effects, particularly among individuals who deal with chronic or long-lasting stressors. Explain some of the detrimental effects of chronic stress, including the following points:

- The increased fatty acids in the bloodstream just "hang around" and can eventually lead to arteriosclerosis (hardening of the arteries). The increased amount of adrenaline (to provide energy) can also damage blood vessel walls.

- The increase in blood pressure can result in hypertension (high blood pressure), strokes, and even heart attacks in vulnerable individuals.

- Elevated levels of lipids (like cholesterol and triglycerides) in the bloodstream can also increase the risk of heart disease and stroke.

- Blood is diverted from the stomach to the legs. The lining of the stomach is not getting enough oxygen and nutrients, and this can result in gastrointestinal problems and ulcers. An increase in the amount of stomach acid can also lead to ulcers.

- When under stress, the immune system (which fights viruses and tumors) doesn't work as well, as seen in a number of studies. For example, one study showed that people who were under stress were more likely to catch a cold than people who were not under stress, even though both groups of people were exposed to the same cold virus (Cohen, Doyle, & Skoner, 1999).

- These hormonal and immunological changes also are typically accompanied by anxiety, depression, loneliness, and social isolation. These psychological effects decrease a person's well-being.

Creating Awareness (20 minutes)

Awareness of Physical Tension

Stress management starts with increasing awareness of both the obvious signs and subtle bodily signals of stress. Awareness of the occurrence of signals of stress and automatic reactions and behaviors is an important first step to making changes. Tell participants that you want them to get to know their sources of stress or stressors and to be able to identify their bodies' reaction as the stress is building so that they can start as early as possible to nip it in the bud.

Body Awareness Exercise

Have group members conduct a body scan from their toes to their heads, including high tension areas like the abdomen, shoulders, back, and neck. Have participants ask themselves the following questions:

- Where am I tight?

- How long has that tension been there?

- Did anything happen or is still happening that is connected with feeling this tension?

Discussion Questions

- "What are your typical sources of tension?"

- "In what part of your body are you most likely to feel this tension?"

- "When are you most likely to feel tense?"

- "When are you most and least aware of bodily tension?"

Power of Thoughts Exercise

Discuss with the group how what we think can affect our mood and physical response. Conduct the following exercise to demonstrate the power of thoughts over our feelings.

Ask participants to get into pairs. One person takes a few moments to think of three words that mean weakness (e.g., weak, fragile, soft). The person then closes his eyes and holds out an arm while repeating those three words over and over. The other member of the pair puts his hand on his partner's arm and tries to pull it down. The exercise is repeated while the person thinks of words that represent strength (e.g., power, confidence, control). The partners then switch roles.

After the exercise, discuss with group members what sensations they felt when repeating words representing weakness versus words representing strength. Note how our thoughts can affect the way we feel physically and emotionally.

Imagery Exercise: Thoughts, Emotions, and Physical Sensations

The following exercise will help participants increase their awareness of physical feelings and emotions felt in connection with their thoughts. Note this exercise may bring up strong emotions; if needed, have participants use diaphragmatic breathing to calm down.

Close your eyes and think of someone you are having difficulty with. (Pause.) *Get a good picture of the person in your mind—his or her face and expression, the color of his or her hair and eyes, the kind of clothes he or she wears, how he or she holds herself. Imagine how his or her voice sounds and how he or she smells. Think about how you feel when you are with him or her. Become aware of the physical sensations in your body. Pay particular attention to your chest and stomach, where we feel a lot of the sensations that are connected with our emotions. Do you feel tight or loose? Open or closed? Do you feel warm inside or have butterflies? Do you have a rising or sinking feeling? Take in all the sensations of your body and think about how they feel.*

Have participants repeat the imagery exercise, but this time thinking of someone they love (or care about a lot).

Have group members describe the physical sensations they felt during the two versions of the imagery exercise. How were they alike? How did they differ? Inquire about what kinds of feelings they were most aware of. They don't have to say anything about the person they imagined or who it is. Don't let participants use generic descriptions such as good, nice, etc. They should use as many descriptive adjectives as possible. Encourage them to identify the sensations as descriptively and idiosyncratically as they can (e.g., "like a snake curled up in my stomach").

Emphasize that as they just experienced, there is a relationship between the way we think and the way we feel. Their thoughts—and not the physical presence of the people they were thinking about—created their emotions and physical sensations. Now, have participants think about how chronic negative thoughts can affect their bodies.

Introduction to the Appraisal Process (10 minutes)

Emotions and Thoughts Are Related

Reinforce the concept that when we feel any emotion such as sadness, anger, or joy, we also experience physical changes and, at the same time, we have thoughts or images. Explain to participants that when we experience an emotion, we actually experience several things with it:

■ We "feel" the emotion—the affect (e.g., anxiety)

■ We experience changes in our bodies (e.g., heart races)

■ We experience thoughts or images (e.g., "The cancer will come back.")

All of these components of emotion are equally important, and they interact to perpetuate one another.

Use the following diagram to demonstrate the appraisal process. The way we feel is a result of how we perceive events around us. Whether we

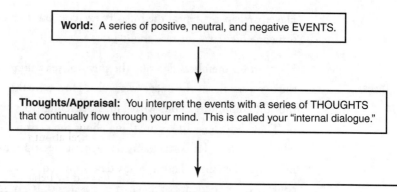

World: A series of positive, neutral, and negative EVENTS.

Thoughts/Appraisal: You interpret the events with a series of THOUGHTS that continually flow through your mind. This is called your "internal dialogue."

Mood: Your feelings are created by your thoughts and not the actual events. All experiences must be processed through your brain and given a conscious meaning before you experience any emotional response.

Figure 4.1

The Appraisal Process

are aware of it or not, every event that we encounter leads to a thinking process or what we call an appraisal. Through this appraisal process, we evaluate the event and an emotional response occurs.

Stages of the Appraisal Process

Review the stages of the appraisal process with the group.

1. *Event:* Something is happening (i.e., a stressor).

2. *Perception:* Your mind becomes aware of this event. The event has to be perceived or filtered in.

3. *Appraisal/Thoughts/Self-Talk:* To experience an emotional state, the event must be appraised for its implication for your personal well-being. After you have perceived the event, you start to determine the impact of this event.

How do you determine the impact of the event? Relevant issues would include:

■ What's happening?

■ Do I care about what's happening?

- Is it good or bad for me?

- Can I do anything about it?

- Can I cope with it?

- Will it get better or worse?

4. *Emotional/Physical State:* What you feel about the event is directly linked with how you appraise it. Emotions are the result of a set of appraisals. Emotions are accompanied by behavioral and physical reactions.

Demonstration of the Appraisal Process

Place the following grid on a flip chart or board and work through an example given by group or the example provided to illustrate the link between events, appraisals, and mood.

Event (stressor)	Perception (becoming aware)	Appraisal (what we think/say to ourselves)	Emotion/Feeling (how we feel/respond)
Expecting a phone call from a friend. He hasn't called.	He was supposed to call me. He is half an hour late. What's happening?	He doesn't care about me. He knows I'm waiting for his call. Nobody is interested in me anymore.	Sad and angry.

Appraisals, Emotions, and Reactions (10 minutes)

The next step of awareness is becoming aware of the relationship among what we think (appraisal), what we feel (emotion), and how we react (physical and behavioral response). We typically do not make these connections during our day-to-day experiences. Refer participants to the Feelings—Back to Basics Chart in the workbook to help them identify common emotions. The chart gives examples of what kinds of situations are associated with certain emotions, characteristic reactions, and typical effects.

Automatic Thoughts

Explain to the group that when we are appraising an event, these thoughts occur so quickly that sometimes they are referred to as *automatic thoughts*. The term "automatic" refers to a stage of a learning process. The more we repeat an action the more we learn to perform it and the faster we learn to do it. After a while it is automatic and we don't even realize we are doing it. Emphasize that the appraisal process is very fast! Use the following examples to illustrate this process.

Driving Example

Think about learning to drive. At the beginning when you see a traffic light, you talk to yourself about what to do . . . It doesn't take time to learn to stop when the light turns red—it becomes AUTOMATIC, like a reflex.

Stress that because it happens so quickly, it is not easy to become aware of what we think about an event.

Swimming Example

Think about improving your performance in any rote skill, that is, any skill that becomes automatic after you practice it awhile. Let's take swimming, for example. In order to improve your style you first have to be AWARE of what you are doing wrong. Because you swam in a certain way so many times, it is now AUTOMATIC and very hard to be AWARE of your movement. One way to be aware of your movement is to videotape yourself and carefully observe what you do. By slowing down the tape you can observe, frame by frame, a very complex process.

Explain that in the same way we can try to find ways to videotape our thoughts. There is no easy way to record our thoughts, self-talk, or appraisals. To identify more easily our thoughts and appraisals, we have to start paying close attention to our emotions. Emotions and physical reactions can be clues to our thoughts.

The Multicomponents of Emotion

Remind participants that when they feel any emotion—sadness, anger, joy, confusion, they have organized certain thoughts or images and they also experience physical changes at the same time. They respond by using coping mechanisms—moving or behaving in a certain way (e.g., being alone or calling a friend).

All of these components of emotion are important and they interact with each other. They are indicators that can help make us *aware* of our emotional state. By paying attention to our thoughts, physical sensations, and behavior, we can become more aware of how we feel. We can also become more aware of what stressors are likely to lead to negative emotions physical sensations, and so forth. Making these connections helps us understand how events in our lives can affect how we feel, both emotionally and physically.

Likewise, our emotions are an indicator that we are appraising something. When we feel an emotion, we can work backward to understand the event, how we appraised the event, and subsequently how this made us feel.

Practicing the Appraisal Process (10 minutes)

Have each group member share at least one example of a situation and its ensuing appraisal process (situation → perception → thoughts → feelings). You can use the following scenarios as examples.

Scenario 1

Situation: *The doctor said that I have prostate cancer.*

Perception: *The doctor just gave me horrible news.*

Thoughts: *I'm going to die. This is going to ruin my life. I'm being punished. Cancer is a death sentence.*

Feelings: *scared, worried, sad*

Scenario 2

Situation: *I'm getting out of the car, and I feel like I can't control my urine.*

Perception: *My pants are getting wet.*

Thoughts: *This sucks! I can't believe that I can't control this. Everyone will see that I peed in my pants.*

Feelings: *embarrassed, ashamed*

Homework (5 minutes)

✎ Have group members review session 2 of the workbook and complete the exercises.

✎ Have group members complete the Stress Monitoring Sheet for at least two stressful situations they encounter in the coming week. If you'd like to provide group members with additional copies, you may photocopy this sheet from the workbook.

✎ Have group members review the Feelings—Back to the Basics Chart in the workbook.

Session Evaluation (5 minutes)(optional)

Have group members complete the session evaluation sheet (see appendix).

Chapter 5

Session 3: Deep Breathing and Counting with Passive Progressive Muscle Relaxation / Sex and Sexuality After Prostate Cancer Treatment and Automatic Thoughts

(Corresponds to session 3 of the workbook)

Materials Needed

- PMR script from session 1
- Flip chart or board
- Copy of participant workbook
- Comfortable chairs for relaxation training
- Copies of relaxation tapes (optional)
- Copies of monitoring sheets (optional)
- Copies of session evaluation sheet (optional)

RELAXATION TRAINING: *Deep Breathing and Counting with Passive Progressive Muscle Relaxation*

Outline

- Discuss adherence to relaxation practice (5 minutes)
- Introduce deep breathing and counting (5 minutes)
- Introduce passive progressive muscle relaxation (5 minutes)

- Conduct deep breathing and counting with passive 4-Muscle-Group PMR (15 minutes)

- Discuss relaxation practice (3 minutes)

- Assign homework (2 minutes)

Discussion of Adherence to Relaxation Practice (5 minutes)

Discuss obstacles or difficulties with relaxation practice. Ask participants the following questions:

- "How often do you find you are able to practice the relaxation exercise?"

- "Where are you practicing relaxation?"

- "What gets in the way for you?"

Optional: collect Relaxation Monitoring Sheets and distribute relaxation tapes.

Introduction to Deep Breathing and Counting (5 minutes)

Tell the group that today they will do two different kinds of relaxation exercises. First, they will repeat the diaphragmatic breathing technique practiced last week, but rather than just breathing in and out, they will count to four while breathing. Tell participants not to worry if they can't hold their breath until the count of four. This is just a way to start slowing the breath and to provide a different sort of focus that may work better for some people. For homework, they should continue practicing whichever of the two breathing exercises they prefer 3–4 times a day. Remind participants that they can do this anywhere—in the car, in line at the supermarket, at work—and it doesn't have to take more than a few minutes.

Do a brief run-through of the new counting exercise:

Now, just sit back and relax in your chair and close your eyes. It often helps if you gently place your hands on your abdomen so you can feel it rising and falling. We will breathe in to the count of 4, hold to the count of 4, exhale to the count of 4, and hold to the count of 4. Breathe in 2 . . . 3 . . . 4 . . . , and hold 2 . . . 3 . . . 4 . . . , exhale 2 . . . 3 . . . 4 . . . , and hold 2 . . . 3 . . . 4. . . . OK, you can open your eyes now.

During today's relaxation session, the group will practice this breathing exercise a few times and then move directly into passive progressive muscle relaxation.

Introduction to Passive Progressive Muscle Relaxation (5 minutes)

Explain to group members that this exercise is called passive relaxation because this time they will not actually be tensing their muscles, but just remembering the feeling associated with the release of tension from a muscle group. They will start by scanning each muscle group for tension and then they will recall the feeling of completely relaxing that muscle group.

Review again the muscle groups used for 4-Muscle-Group PMR. To remind participants of the feelings of tension and relaxation, have them go through the muscle groups and briefly tense and relax each one.

1. Arms

2. Legs

3. Stomach, Chest, Shoulders and Upper Back

4. Neck, Mouth, Jaw, and Throat

Reiterate that when performing today's exercise, participants will not actually be tensing and releasing the muscles, but just remembering the feeling of tension and release from tension.

Deep Breathing and Counting with Passive 4-Muscle-Group PMR (15 minutes)

Use the following scripts to conduct the combined exercise. Move directly from the deep breathing and counting exercise into passive 4-Muscle-Group PMR.

Deep Breathing and Counting

Just get comfortable and close your eyes. Gently place your hands on your abdomen and start by taking a few deep breaths. Feel your hands rise and fall with each inhalation and exhalation. Breathe in through your nose, feeling the cool air coming in . . . and breathe out through your mouth, feeling the warm air whooshing out.

Breathe in . . . 2 . . . 3 . . . 4 . . . and hold . . . 2 . . . 3 . . . 4 . . . and out . . . 2 . . . 3 . . . 4 . . . and hold . . . 2 . . . 3 . . . 4. (Continue counting aloud to the group for several more breaths.) *Just allow yourself to settle into a rhythm of breathing that is comfortable to you.*

Passive 4-Muscle-Group PMR

In conducting passive PMR, you will follow the script used during session 1 with the adaptations made for last week's 4-Muscle-Group PMR session. However, remind participants that when you tell them to tense the various muscle groups (you will read the script for these 4 muscle groups verbatim), that they are *not* to tense the muscles, but instead, simply remember what that tension felt like and then continue to relax the muscles as instructed. You may want to end the exercise with the script for whole body relaxation (see session 1).

Post-Relaxation Discussion Questions (3 minutes)

- "What did you like?"

- "What didn't you like?"

- "What aspects were hard/easy for you?"

- "Can you practice this at home using the instructions in the workbook?"

Homework (2 minutes)

■ Have group members practice deep breathing and counting with passive PMR at least once a day. They should record stress levels before and after each practice on the Relaxation Monitoring Sheet.

STRESS MANAGEMENT: *Sex and Sexuality After Prostate Cancer Treatment and Automatic Thoughts*

Facilitator Note

■ *The stress management didactic portion of this session is intentionally shorter to provide ample time for discussion of sex and sexuality issues.* ■

Outline

■ Check in with group members (5 minutes)

■ Discuss sex and sexuality after prostate cancer treatment (10 minutes)

■ Encourage expansion of sexual repertoire (10 minutes)

■ Discuss HIV and how to protect oneself (5 minutes)

■ Review material and homework from previous session (5 minutes)

■ Discuss the functions of emotion/self-talk linkage (5 minutes)

■ Teach how to break the cycle of negative thoughts and feelings (10 minutes)

■ Discuss linking exercise (5 minutes)

■ Assign homework (5 minutes)

■ Have group members complete session evaluation sheet (5 minutes) (optional)

Pre-Didactic Check-In (5 minutes)

Go around the room and have each group member share how he is doing and update other group members on any personal news.

Sex and Sexuality After Prostate Cancer Treatment (10 minutes)

You may want to start the discussion on sex and sexuality after prostate cancer treatment with the following dialogue:

> *Many men who have had prostate cancer, especially those who have had radical prostatectomies, have questions and concerns about sex and sexuality. Some men wonder if they will ever return to the same level of sexual functioning they had before. We are going to address a number of concerns, but it is also important to remember that not everything we say applies to every man.*

Review the following common sexual side effects of cancer treatment with the group. For more information see the American Cancer Society Web Site, www.cancer.org.

Common Effects of Cancer Treatment

- Lack of desire is a common occurrence following treatment, but it is usually temporary.

- Fatigue and pain are common barriers to sexual desire.

- If there is a conflict in the relationship, one partner or both might lose interest in sex.

- Any emotion or thought that keeps a man from feeling excited can also interfere with his getting or keeping an erection.

- The most common anxiety is a nagging fear of not being able to get an erection or satisfy a partner.

Common Physical Changes

After surgery (radical prostatectomy), a man may still have the desire to have sex, but due to surgery-related damage to nerves around the prostate, it is likely that he will not be able to have an erection. Full recovery is possible for only some men, and it takes up to 1 year after surgery. Most men make the most gains in about 12 months after treatment, and these gains are not likely to reach the level of pre-surgery functioning; therefore, some dysfunction is likely to be permanent. Overall, most men will continue to experience sexual desire but will also have erectile dysfunction.

Damage to the nerves due to surgery interferes with blood flow to the penis, and adequate blood flow is necessary to achieve an erection. It is difficult for surgeons to see and spare these nerves since they surround the entire prostate gland. The nerves lie near the rectum and fan out like a cobweb around the prostate. Nerve-sparing procedures involve careful attention to avoiding damage to these nerves. However, many factors such as size of the tumor determine whether nerves can be spared, and even so, sexual dysfunction will still occur at some level.

After surgery, most men will be able to have a partial erection; however, the sensation and ability to achieve an orgasm will remain. Since the prostate gland which produces seminal fluid has been removed, no semen is ejaculated and the orgasm is "dry." Even among men who achieve orgasms, it is not uncommon for their orgasms to be weaker than before surgery. As part of the normal aging process, the intensity of orgasm declines. With prostatectomy, further weakening of the intensity of orgasm will occur. Again, this is related to tissue damage around the prostate gland which involves nerves associated with the sensations of an orgasm.

Psychological Effects of Treatment

A diagnosis of cancer or any invasive medical procedure such as a prostatectomy can cause a series of emotional reactions. These reactions can include fears about recurrence, self-image issues, performance anxiety, shame, and guilt. These feelings can also lead to erectile dysfunction. Because prostatectomy itself leads to problems with erections, negative emotional reactions can make matters worse and lead to further decline in sexual functioning.

Rather than being relaxed and enjoying a sexual encounter, the man treated with prostatectomy may be over-vigilant and anxious, thus leading to performance difficulties. The poor sexual functioning that is exacerbated by anxiety is then interpreted by the man as a self-fulfilling prophecy, in which he believes that he is not meant to have sex since he cannot function.

The reality is that if he is able to gain control of his anxiety and just relax, he will likely achieve a partial erection and an orgasm. Therefore, the more the man feels he can have some control over his body and can relax, the more confidence he will have in his ability to function and eventually will be able to enjoy sexual relations with his partner.

Things to Address with a Physician

- Viagra®

- Injections

- Pumps or vacuum erection device

- Penile "prostheses" or implants

- Sex therapy for psychological barriers to intimacy

Discussion

- "Does anyone have any comments about the information we just presented?"

- "How has everyone been coping with the physical changes they've experienced following surgery?"

Stress to the group that communication is probably the most important part of good sexual relationships. If a man reacts to cancer by withdrawing into himself because he thinks his partner would be burdened by sharing fear or sadness, he forces his partner to cope with the pain alone.

Expanding One's Sexual Repertoire (Who Says You Can't Teach an Old Dog New Tricks) (10 minutes)

This section encourages participants to expand their sexual repertoires and learn how to derive pleasure from alternative sexual activities. You may use the following dialogue to begin:

After cancer, your sexual habits may need to change. For example, if you are unable to get an erection, you will need to learn other ways of loving one another. This is the time for open communication. Do not let your fear of embarrassment prevent you from having an enjoyable and fulfilling sexual experience with your partner. Who says you can't teach an old dog new tricks? There are lots of techniques to try and have fun with.

Sexual Repertoire Exercise

Before beginning the exercise, tell participants that during the course of this program, they will learn that their thoughts influence their feelings and their feelings influence how they act. These strong connections between thoughts, feelings, and actions are also very important in relation to sexuality. In fact, sexual triumphs or tribulations relate much more to how one *thinks* about sexual circumstances than to what *actually happens* "between the sheets." Start the exercise off with the following questions:

- "What is *sex?*"

- "How do you define *sex?*"

- "Think of all of the different things that you can do with a sexual partner that you would consider as *sex*. What are these?"

Use the Sexual Repertoire Worksheet to guide the group discussion on the definition of sex. List various sexual activities on the board. Encourage participants to generate a broad array of sexual activities. Write them on the board as each participant calls out a sexual behavior or activity. Be sure to include any activity that participants define as "sexual." The idea is to move *away* from conventional definitions of sexual behavior. Use the list on the Sexual Repertoire Worksheet to fold in additional sexual behaviors not included by the group. Wrap up the exercise with the following dialogue:

> As you have just discovered, there is much more to sex than the "traditional" definition of intercourse. You may have been conditioned to believe that certain sexual practices are right or wrong, better or worse, allowable or not allowable. Most of us have been brought up to think that intercourse is the ultimate intimate sexual act. However, you can accept this idea less and less and begin to think of intercourse as but one option among many different sexual choices. We call this variety of sexual choices your "sexual repertoire." We will talk more about sexual repertoires throughout this session.

Alternative Sexual Activities and Performance Anxiety Risk

Facilitator Note

■ *Refer to the Sexual Repertoire Worksheet as needed to gain an understanding of alternative sexual activities.* ■

This discussion is designed to prompt an expansion of perceived pleasure derived from alternate sexual behaviors. Encourage participants to identify those behaviors that pose lower risk of rejection or performance anxiety (such as cuddling, dry kissing, and speaking warmly and/or sexually). Have them suggest alternative ways of feeling close, connected, and/or intimate with sexual partners. Remember to be sensitive to cultural and religious beliefs regarding sexual practices. Also distinguish between different types of problems encountered depending on relationship status (e.g., single, married, divorced, widowed).

Have participants turn to the Sexual Repertoire Worksheet in the workbook and rate each of the sexual activities for performance anxiety risk. Then ask the following questions:

- "Which of the sexual activities within the Sexual Repertoire do you consider *lowest risk* for performance anxiety?"

- "Which of the sexual activities within the Sexual Repertoire do you consider *moderate (or "medium") risk* for performance anxiety?"

- "Which of the sexual activities within the Sexual Repertoire do you consider *highest risk* for performance anxiety?"

End this exercise with a discussion of how a man might address the need to try alternative sexual practices with his partner. For example:

I feel ready for sex again, but I'd like to take things slowly. Would you be in the mood tonight to try a little touching? I can't promise that it will go smoothly, but we can have fun trying.

HIV in Older Adults (5 minutes)

Use the following information to discuss HIV with the group.

The Basics

HIV stands for the human immunodeficiency virus, the virus that causes AIDS, or acquired immune deficiency syndrome. Once infected with the virus, a person's immune system ceases to function properly, and the body can no longer fight off diseases and other infections. HIV/AIDS is spread by exchanging blood, semen, and vaginal secretions. This means that HIV can be spread through sexual intercourse or oral sex. HIV is transmitted by having sex or sharing needles with an infected person. Some people contracted HIV prior to 1985 through blood transfusion. One cannot get HIV from giving blood, from using toilet seats or water fountains, by caring for an infected person, or through casual contact. Young people are not the only ones who get infected with HIV. In fact, heterosexual transmission in older adults is increasing. Up to 19% of all AIDS cases in the US are people over the age of 50. (Source: Florida Department of Health, 2005).

How to Protect Oneself

Abstaining from all sexual activity is the only *sure* way to fully protect oneself from HIV. However, this is not realistic for most people. A person should always use a condom when having sexual intercourse if the person does not know whether his partner has been tested for HIV. In addition, needles should never be shared with others.

Previous Material and Homework Review (5 minutes)

Briefly review the main points from last session's stress management section. Answer any questions group members may have.

Review assigned stress management homework (e.g., Stress Monitoring Sheet). Problem-solve any difficulties group members had completing the homework.

Emotion/Self-Talk Linkage (5 minutes)

Last session introduced the concept of automatic thoughts/self-talk. This session focuses on how self-talk is linked to emotions. Explain to the group that each emotion is hypothesized to have its own core pattern of self-talk. Emotions and their self-talk patterns can have important functions for us. If our thinking is accurate, then our emotions will probably be accurate as well. Refer to Table 5.1 (a copy of this chart is also found in the participant workbook) and note how sadness, anger, guilt, and anxiety have different self-talk patterns and specific functions. These patterns are helpful when thoughts accurately match the situation.

After reviewing the chart with group members, explain that we often experience these emotional reactions *unnecessarily* because we have adopted preconceived, and perhaps mistaken, patterns of response to certain situations. That is, if we have an automatic thought that is inaccurate because we are misinterpreting a situation, we tend to unnecessarily experience these negative emotions. Subsequently, the negative emotions perpetuate a cycle of negative thoughts and we are trapped in this vicious cycle needlessly.

Table 5.1 Examples of Emotion/Self-Talk Linkage

Feelings	Thoughts/Self-Talk	Function
SADNESS	Poor me! I have lost something important. There is nothing I can do.	Prepares and motivates you to grieve and to reinvest in something else.
ANGER	This is not OK. This is wrong! This is someone else's fault. It should not be like this. I'll show them!	Prepares and motivates you to achieve a goal and remove barriers or to protect yourself.
GUILT	I am not OK. I am wrong. I should have . . . . Could I do something to fix it?	Motivates you to adhere to personal and social norms.
ANXIETY	I am in danger. Something bad could happen to me. I'd better go and prepare to fight or escape fast.	Prepares and motivates you to meet a challenge or to escape danger.

Breaking the Vicious Cycle (10 minutes)

Emphasize to the group that events can be interpreted in such a way that they can create unnecessary emotional distress. These distressing feelings have self-talk patterns that help perpetuate these feelings. For example:

A man goes to his oncologist for a follow-up prostate specific antigen (PSA) test and thinks about the possibility of having a recurrence; consequently, he feels more anxiety, and his heart races. He notices his heart racing (AWARENESS) and thinks he is unable to control it (APPRAISAL), which creates more anxiety. He then thinks, "I'm so anxious, I'm sure they'll find something wrong" (APPRAISAL). This leads to even more anxiety and on it goes. Pretty soon, he feels like he can't control his emotions.

Explain that the easiest place to break the cycle is at the level of thoughts and images. How a person interprets events determines how he feels about them. So, in this example the man could break the cycle by changing his negative thoughts to something more like, "I don't know whether or not there is anything wrong. I have been taking good care of myself and having regular check-ups. If they do find something, I will deal with one thing at a time." A thought like this will lead to less anxiety, so he will feel more comfortable about taking the PSA test.

Steps to Breaking the Cycle

Remind participants that these thoughts occur so quickly that we refer to them as *automatic*. Explain that once they learn to identify negative thought patterns, they can work on changing them to more accurate and balanced ones. With practice, these more balanced appraisals can become automatic. Review the following steps to breaking the cycle with the group:

Step 1) Become AWARE of negative thinking patterns.

Step 2) Learn to RECOGNIZE anxiety-producing APPRAISALS. (Can use physical signs as cues.)

Step 3) Begin to NOTICE that these thoughts are AUTOMATIC.

Step 4) Take note that these thoughts are often NEGATIVE or DISTORTED.

Step 5) Begin to CHANGE thoughts to more BALANCED APPRAISALS.

The following example can be used to demonstrate the change from negative, inaccurate thoughts to more balanced appraisals.

Example

Situation: *The doctor's office left a message on the answering machine asking you to call them back.*

Old automatic thought: *Something is wrong!*

New thought: *I don't know if there is something wrong. I am checked frequently and all has been well. I will not jump to conclusions until I talk with my doctor.*

Facilitator Note

■ *A lighthearted comment to add here is that the office might have called to ask about the bill.* ■

Linking Exercise (5 minutes)

Tell group members they have now seen how self-talk affects their emotions. In coming sessions, they will also be focusing on their behavior. Use an example from the group session to generate an example of the link between awareness, appraisals, emotions, and behavior. Draw a grid on the board with four headings: Awareness, Appraisals, Emotions, and Behavior. Or, use the following example:

Awareness	Appraisals	Emotions	Behavior
See an attractive woman and think about what it would be like to have sex with her.	I'll never be able to do that again because my equipment doesn't work.	I feel inadequate and depressed.	I won't approach her.

Briefly discuss with the group about how more balanced appraisals can affect our behavior. If the man in the example felt more confident, he might have approached the attractive woman. This would not necessarily lead to a sexual relationship, but it could challenge the distortion that the woman would not be interested in him because of sexual dysfunction. Stress that sex is important in relationships, but it is just one component that makes relationships work. There are many other characteristics of a man that attract a woman as well. If the man in the example had this kind of balanced thought, he would be more likely to approach the woman.

Homework (5 minutes)

✎ Have group members review session 3 of the workbook.

✎ Have group members review the Sexual Repertoire Worksheet.

✎ Have group members complete the Stress Awareness Monitoring Sheet for two separate stressful events they encounter in the next week. If you'd like to provide group members with additional copies, you may photocopy this sheet from the workbook.

Session Evaluation (5 minutes)(optional)

Have group members complete the session evaluation sheet (see appendix).

Chapter 6 | *Session 4: Special Place Imagery / Cognitive Distortions*

(Corresponds to session 4 of the workbook)

Materials Needed

- PMR script from session 1
- Flip chart or board
- Copy of participant workbook
- Comfortable chairs for relaxation training
- Copies of relaxation tapes (optional)
- Copies of monitoring sheets (optional)
- Copies of scssion evaluation sheet (optional)

RELAXATION TRAINING: *Special Place Imagery*

Outline

- Discuss adherence to relaxation practice (5 minutes)
- Introduce special place imagery (5 minutes)
- Conduct passive PMR with special place imagery exercise (20 minutes)
- Discuss relaxation practice (3 minutes)
- Assign homework (2 minutes)

Discussion of Adherence to Relaxation Practice (5 minutes)

Discuss obstacles or difficulties with relaxation practice. Ask the following questions:

- "Have you noticed any benefits yet?"

- "Have you encountered any barriers to conducting the relaxation?"

- "Has anyone encountered similar barriers but has been able to make adjustments and conduct the exercise? Can these be shared with the group?"

Optional: collect Relaxation Monitoring Sheets and distribute relaxation tapes.

Introduction to Special Place Imagery (5 minutes)

This session introduces the use of imagery, and in particular, imagery associated with a special place. Explain that the Special Place Imagery Exercise is a deep passive relaxation experience, in which participants combine the images of a previously selected special place with the images you suggest to create a calming effect.

Prepare for the exercise by having group members think of a special place—a place they have been, or have seen in a movie or a picture, or an imaginary place—where they feel calm and safe (e.g., rain forest, mountain, lake house, a special room at home). When they have selected a place, they are ready to begin the relaxation experience. You may want to tell participants that, if they want to, they may change the place during the exercise.

Passive PMR with Special Place Imagery Exercise (20 minutes)

To conduct this relaxation exercise, first take participants through passive PMR (using the instructions provided in session 3), and then without stopping, move immediately into the Special Place Imagery Exercise (using the following script). This allows group members to gain the benefits of both procedures during the same relaxation session.

Passive PMR

Remind participants that when you tell them to tense the various muscle groups (you will read the script for these four muscle groups from session 1 verbatim), they are *not* to tense the muscles, but instead, simply remember what that tension felt like and then continue to relax the muscles as instructed.

Special Place Imagery Script

Allow yourself to become comfortable and gently focus on your breathing. Notice how you can achieve a rhythm of breathing, deeper and deeper, slower and slower, becoming more and more relaxed with every breath . . . just allow yourself to slow down. Slowly, gently, calmly, breathe in and out.

As you breathe in you can mentally say to yourself a word like "relax" or any phrase that will help you just let go and bring yourself to a deeper state of calm and peace.

As you breathe out, you can let go of all your tension, all your stress . . . just let it go and let it leave your body. With every exhalation, let the tension go, allowing yourself to become more and more relaxed.

Focus on your breath gently, quietly. Watch the breathing in and out. If you notice thoughts going by, it's okay. Just notice them as they drift by. As you continue to breathe slowly and deeply, you may notice feelings of comfort and warmth.

Allow yourself to breathe in the comfort and calm your body experiences in a relaxed state. As you are feeling completely relaxed, imagine a place, a special place that you enjoy, where you feel peaceful, calm, and relaxed. It may be a place where you feel secure and safe, or where you have experienced a sense of beauty, joy, or awe. . . .

Imagine yourself going to your special place now in your mind. Let yourself be in that place now. Breathe deeply and feel its peace. . . . Feel that place begin to fill you with a deep sense of calm and joy. Look around you. See the shapes and colors of your special place. Can you see the sun? What are the textures that you see? What do you hear? Smell the air. Can you feel its freshness? What is the temperature? Do you feel a cool breeze against your face? Be aware of all the sensations in your special place. Feel the peace of your special place.

Breathe in, and as you breathe in, let yourself be completely filled with the serenity of this special place. Allow yourself to experience its beauty. Let it nourish and calm you. Go over these different sensations again allowing yourself to become more and more relaxed. With every breath, let the calmness spread deeper through your body . . . restoring every cell, bringing energy, healing, relaxing wholeness throughout your body.

[Pause for 1 minute]

Breathe in the calm deeper and deeper, letting it fill you. Know that this is a place you always have inside of you. And that you have the ability to go there any time you want by breathing deeply in and out, gently closing your eyes, and taking yourself to this inner healing place.

Now, I am going to count from 4 to 1. When I say 4, you can begin to move your feet and toes. When I say 3, you can begin to move your arms and hands. When I count to 2, you can begin to move your head and neck. And on 1, you can stretch and gradually open your eyes, coming to a fully alert state, but retaining the calm and peace of this relaxation experience.
4 . . . 3 . . . 2 . . . 1.

Post-Relaxation Discussion (3 minutes)

- "Was passive PMR easier this session than last?"
- "How did this new imagery exercise feel?"
- "Were you able to imagine your special place?"
- "Did it have a relaxing effect on your body?"

Explain to participants that the goal of introducing different relaxation exercises is to help them find the technique that works best for them. One is not necessarily superior to the other. For example, some may prefer to do only deep breathing while others favor tensing and relaxing the muscles.

Homework (2 minutes)

✎ Have group members practice passive PMR and special place imagery at least once a day. They should record stress levels before and after each practice on the Relaxation Monitoring Sheet.

STRESS MANAGEMENT: *Cognitive Distortions*

Outline

- ▪ Check in with group members (5 minutes)

- ▪ Review material and homework from the previous session (5 minutes)

- ▪ Introduce types of negative thinking/cognitive distortions (10 minutes)

- ▪ Discuss how negative thoughts influence behavior (5 minutes)

- ▪ Have group members practice labeling negative thoughts (10 minutes)

- ▪ Review possible areas of negative thoughts (5 minutes)

- ▪ Conduct group discussion on negative thoughts (10 minutes)

- ▪ Discuss changing negative thoughts about sexuality (5 minutes)

- ▪ Assign homework (5 minutes)

- ▪ Have group members complete session evaluation sheet (5 minutes) (optional)

Pre-Didactic Check-In (5 minutes)

Go around the room and have each group member share how he is doing and update other group members on any personal news.

Previous Material and Homework Review (5 minutes)

Answer residual questions about sexual education from the last session. Review the steps to breaking the cycle of negative automatic thoughts and emotions.

Review assigned stress management homework (e.g., Stress Awareness Monitoring Sheet). Problem-solve any difficulties group members had completing the homework.

Negative Thinking/Cognitive Distortions (10 minutes)

Explain to the group that if our perceptions and cognitive appraisals about stressors are accurate, then our emotions will probably be appropriate to the situation. If our appraisals are distorted or inaccurate, then our emotions will probably be extreme or off base as well. This is often how depression, anxiety, anger, guilt and stress in general occur unnecessarily. However, this does not mean that we experience negative emotions only when our appraisals are distorted. Remind the group that emotions can accurately match a situation and indicate that action needs to be taken. Often our thinking is a mixture of accurate and distorted appraisals.

Negative thinking often involves inaccurate appraisals, which are commonly used by most people at one time or another. Introduce some of the most common types of inaccurate appraisals and some familiar negative thoughts that correspond with them. These are adapted from *Feeling Good: The New Mood Therapy* (Burns, 1981).

All-or-Nothing Thinking (Black-and-White Thinking)

You think in black and white terms; there are no in-betweens or gray areas. Perfectionism is often the result of this kind of thinking. You are afraid to make any mistakes, because if you are not perfect then you see yourself as a complete failure. This type of thinking is unrealistic because things are rarely all good or all bad. An example of this type of thinking is "Real men never cry, and I cried, so I must not be a real man."

Overgeneralization

You see a single negative event as part of a pattern of defeat. You conclude that something that happened to you once will occur over and over again. For example, you might say, "Now that I have developed prostate cancer all my children and grandchildren are doomed to have cancer too;" "If I have one episode of erectile dysfunction, I will never be able to have sex again."

Mental Filter

You pick out a single negative detail and focus on it so much that you can't see anything positive. When you are depressed you see the world through special glasses that darken your entire view of reality. Only the negative things get through, and since you don't realize that you are filtering out the positive, you assume that there is nothing positive and everything really is negative. For example, you have a review at work and your boss gives you some criticism as well as praise. Afterward, the only thing you can think about is the criticism.

Disqualifying the Positive

You discount any positive experiences so you can continue believing that things are completely negative. This kind of thinking is very harmful, since you cannot be convinced that you have any value no matter what happens. An example of this would be if a woman tells her partner that she has enjoyed a sexual interaction with him (such as caressing or mutual masturbation), and the man thinks she is just saying this to make him feel better.

Jumping to Conclusions

In the absence of solid evidence, you jump to a negative conclusion. There are two types of this: "mind reading" and the "fortune teller error."

Mind Reading

You assume that you know what someone else is thinking. You are so convinced that someone is having a negative reaction to you, you don't even take the time to confirm your guess. For example, you see an acquaintance at a party and she doesn't come over to talk, you think, "She's avoiding me because she knows I have prostate cancer." It's possible, however, that she was just caught up in conversation with someone else.

Fortune Teller Error

You act as a fortune teller who only predicts the worst for you. You then treat your prediction as if it were a proven fact. For example: "I've had prostate cancer. I'm going to have a recurrence and die real soon" vs. "I might never have a recurrence and worrying won't change the future. I can make the most of each day and learn to lead a healthier life. "

Magnification (Catastrophizing) or Minimization

You magnify the importance of negative things (e.g., errors you made at work) and minimize the significance of positive things (e.g., your own accomplishments). It's as if you are looking through either the small or large end of binoculars.

An example of magnification is, "I do not function sexually as I used to. Now my partner will not love me as before my treatment!" You are catastrophizing your situation, as if you were looking through binoculars that make your problems look larger than they really are.

Minimization occurs when you look at your strengths and good points and minimize their significance, as if you were looking through the wrong end of the binoculars. For example, you think, "I did a good job, but it's not a big deal. Anyone could have done it."

Emotional Reasoning

You let your negative emotions convince you that how you feel is the way things really are. For example: "I feel guilty, therefore I deserve this" or "I feel depressed, therefore I'm a loser." Since your feelings reflect your thoughts and beliefs, which may be distorted, these emotions may have little validity. Emotional reasoning plays a role in keeping some people depressed; things *feel* so negative they assume they truly are.

"Should" Statements

You try to motivate yourself with "shoulds," "musts," and "oughts," as if you had to be reprimanded before you could be expected to do anything. Guilt is the result of this kind of thinking. When you use these statements toward others, it can cause you to feel anger, frustration, and resentment. Common examples are, "I must be able to handle my condition all by myself" or "I should not ask for help" or "If people care about me, they ought to be able to tell I need help."

Labeling and Mislabeling

Personal labeling means creating a completely negative self-image based on one mistake. Instead of describing your actions ("I did something stupid"), you attach a negative label to yourself ("I'm stupid"). When someone else's behavior bothers you, you attach a negative label to him ("He's a jerk"). Mislabeling involves describing an event with language that is emotionally extreme. For example: "The meeting was a total waste of time."

Personalization

You see yourself as the cause of some negative external event for which in fact you were not primarily responsible. You arbitrarily decide that a negative occurrence is your fault or reflects your inadequacy. Personalization causes you to feel guilt: "My lover is depressed, and it's my fault."

Cognitive Distortions and Behavior (5 minutes)

Discuss with the group how these types of negative thoughts may influence our behavior. We may respond to these inaccurate appraisals with:

- Withdrawal: becoming unsociable, withdrawn, depressed

- Some type of counterattack: acting defensive, taking out your negative feelings on others

This kind of self-defeating behavior pattern may act as a *self-fulfilling prophecy* and set up a negative interaction in a relationship when there wasn't one in the first place.

Labeling Negative Thoughts (10 minutes)

This next exercise is designed to help participants label the negative automatic thoughts people sometimes have. Remind the group that sometimes our negative thoughts involve more than one type of thinking error. Go over each example and prompt for the cognitive distortions involved.

1. *You feel particularly tired after a long day. You think, "The cancer must be back. I probably only have a week to live." The thinking errors involve what types of negative thinking?*

Cognitive Distortions: Magnifying, Fortune-telling, Jumping to conclusions

2. *You run into a friend who immediately asks you how you are feeling. You say, "He must think I look pretty bad or otherwise he wouldn't have asked about my health. The cancer must really be taking its toll on my physical appearance." What types of distortions are involved with these self-statements?*

Cognitive Distortions: Disqualifying the positive, Jumping to conclusions, Mind reading

3. *Recently, an additional person has been hired to perform similar duties to yours. You say to yourself, "I am being replaced; I need this job; if I was any good at my job, they wouldn't need anyone else." Can you identify any cognitive distortions in this self-talk?*

Cognitive Distortions: Jumping to conclusions, Catastrophizing

Finally, have group members look at examples of negative thoughts from their Stress Awareness Monitoring Sheets they completed for homework. Ask them if they can recognize any themes underlying their negative thinking.

Areas of Negative Thoughts (5 minutes)

Review possible areas where negative thoughts can occur. These include:

■ Family relationships

■ Support network (e.g., friends, acquaintances)

■ Going to your oncologist for a check-up

■ Quality of health care

■ Job responsibilities

Have group members generate additional areas in which automatic negative thoughts are common. You may want to list these on a flip chart or blackboard.

Group Discussion (10 minutes)

Have group members discuss their favorite/most common negative thoughts:

■ "Which type of negative thought did you identify with the most?"

■ "Think about a specific situation where you were last anxious or depressed. What were you thinking during that situation? Any examples of negative thinking?"

You should give your own examples to get the ball rolling. You can tell the group that this week they will focus on identifying negative thoughts, and then next week they will learn a method for refuting irrational thoughts.

Identifying Negative Thoughts

For additional practice, have group members complete the exercise in the workbook entitled "Identifying Negative Thoughts."

Changing Negative Thoughts About Sexuality (5 minutes)

Participants can also apply the techniques they've learned for reducing stress in their everyday lives to their sexuality. Use the following example to demonstrate:

> Saying "A man who can't have erections is no good at all in bed" is black-and-white thinking. You can reframe the situation by thinking "Even though I cannot achieve a full erection, I am able to satisfy my lover through other methods."

Identifying Negative Automatic Thoughts and Sexuality

Have the group practice identifying negative thoughts about sexuality by using the following example:

> Jim thinks that his partner is disinterested in having sex since his prostatectomy. He thinks to himself, "She is not interested in having sex with me. She never touches me anymore, so she must not find me attractive. We have not had sex/enough sex. Our relationship is falling apart. Soon, I'll be alone."

Draw two columns on the board as follows. List the negative thoughts and have group members identify the cognitive distortions.

Negative Thoughts	Cognitive Distortions
"Partner is disinterested."	Jumping to Conclusions
"She doesn't think I'm attractive."	Mind reading
"Our relationship is falling apart."	Catastrophizing
"She will leave me."	Fortune-telling

Have group members come up with ways Jim can reframe the situation and have more balanced appraisals. Point out how a more balanced thinking approach avoids running into the common cognitive distortions.

Homework (5 minutes)

✎ Have group members review session 4 of the workbook and complete the exercises.

✎ Have group members complete the Cognitive Distortions Monitoring Sheet for two separate stressful events they encounter in the next week. If you'd like to provide group members with additional copies, you may photocopy this sheet from the workbook.

Session Evaluation (5 minutes) (optional)

Have group members complete the session evaluation sheet (see appendix).

Chapter 7 | *Session 5: Relaxation for Healing and Well-Being / Cognitive Restructuring*

(Corresponds to session 5 of the workbook)

Materials Needed

- Flip chart or board

- Copy of participant workbook

- Comfortable chairs for relaxation training

- Copies of relaxation tapes (optional)

- Copies of monitoring sheets (optional)

- Copies of session evaluation sheet (optional)

RELAXATION TRAINING: *Relaxation for Healing and Well-Being*

Outline

- Discuss adherence to relaxation practice (5 minutes)

- Introduce relaxation exercise for healing and well-being (5 minutes)

- Conduct relaxation exercise (15 minutes)

- Discuss relaxation exercise (3 minutes)

- Assign homework (2 minutes)

Discussion of Adherence to Relaxation Practice (5 minutes)

Discuss obstacles or difficulties with relaxation practice. Ask the following questions:

■ "How do you find you are using the relaxation techniques?"

■ "Do breathing and relaxation exercises give you more time to come up with more balanced thoughts?"

■ "When are these techniques not working?"

■ "When could you be using them that you're not?"

Optional: collect Relaxation Monitoring Sheets and distribute relaxation tapes.

Introduction to Relaxation Exercise for Healing and Well-Being (5 minutes)

In the past couple of decades, much has been written on the benefits of visualization in coping with cancer. Beginning in the early 1970s, proponents of visualization suggested that different techniques improve people's chances of feeling better after cancer (Simonton, 1978). Since any form of relaxation has beneficial effects on a person's psychological and physiological stress response, such techniques may be very helpful if used on a regular basis. Today the group will do an exercise to promote healing and well-being, which will include relaxation breathing and visualization.

Relaxation Exercise for Healing and Well-Being (15 minutes)

This basic script can be expanded on as time allows. (Adapted from Hadley & Staudacher, 1996)

Just get comfortable and close your eyes. Gently place your hands on your abdomen and start by taking a few deep breaths. As you feel your hands rise and fall with each breath, begin to relax. Take a moment to notice the rhythm of your breathing: in . . . and out . . . in . . . and out.

As you become more and more relaxed, you may find yourself taking more notice of any noise around you. Just take note of these sounds and bring your attention back to your breathing. Anything you hear will begin to sound far away and will only help to relax you.

Inhale and as you exhale, release any stress from any part of your body. Let go of any stressful feelings you may have. Feel the thoughts rushing through your mind begin to wind down.

Think about relaxing every muscle in your body, from the top of your head, to the tips of your toes. As you relax each part of your body, feel yourself drifting further and further down into a state of deep relaxation.

Now imagine a healing light circulating throughout your whole body. This light heals and cleanses every organ, nerve, muscle, and cell of your body. Feel the light's gentle warmth as it flows through every part of your body, cleansing and healing over and over again.

Now imagine yourself healthy and strong. You feel wonderful, healthy, and strong. This feeling will continue throughout the day and into the night. Each day, you will feel stronger and stronger.

Continue relaxing and enjoy the positive sense of well-being you have created. In a few moments, I'll begin counting from four to one and you will come back feeling refreshed and alert. FOUR, begin to gently move your legs and feet; THREE, begin to gently move your arms and hands; TWO, begin to gently move your head and neck; and ONE, stretch gently, if you like, and open your eyes.

Post-Relaxation Discussion Questions (3 minutes)

- "How was this exercise for you?"
- "Were you able to imagine a healing light?"
- "Did you feel any impact on your sense of well-being?"

Homework (2 minutes)

✎ Have group members practice the relaxation exercise for healing and well-being at least once a day. They should record stress levels before and after each practice on the Relaxation Monitoring Sheet.

Outline

- Check in with group members (5 minutes)

- Review material and homework from previous session (5 minutes)

- Introduce irrational, rational, and rationalized thoughts (10 minutes)

- Have group members practice identifying self-talk (10 minutes)

- Conduct role play of irrational, rational, and rationalized responses (5 minutes)

- Teach how to replace negative thoughts with more rational responses (10 minutes)

- Have group practice the steps to thought replacement (10 minutes)

- Review helpful guidelines for generating rational responses (5 minutes)

- Assign homework (5 minutes)

- Have group members complete session evaluation sheet (5 minutes) (optional)

Pre-Didactic Check-In (5 minutes)

Go around the room and have each group member share how he is doing and update other group members on any personal news.

Previous Material and Homework Review (5 minutes)

Review the list of cognitive distortions presented in the last session. Also briefly re-examine the relationship between automatic thoughts, emotions, physical symptoms, and behaviors.

Review homework, including the Cognitive Distortions Monitoring Sheet. Ask what distortions group members noticed using in the last week and how this made them feel. Problem-solve any difficulties group members had completing the homework.

Introduction to Irrational, Rational, and Rationalized Thoughts (10 minutes)

So far the group has been focusing on identifying distorted thoughts. Now that participants know how to become aware of, identify, and label these thoughts, they can learn how to go about changing them. First, present the three general categories our thoughts fall into: irrational, rationalized, and rational self-talk (Figure 7.1).

◄---IRRATIONAL----------RATIONAL----------RATIONALIZED---►

| (pessimistic, negative, self-defeating) | (reasonable, realistic, balanced perception of reality) | (deny concern, distorted thought with an avoidant, falsely optimistic turn) |

Figure 7.1

Types of Self-Talk

Irrational Self-Talk

This type of thinking is inaccurate, negative, or distorted. These thoughts tend to have catastrophic, absolutist, illogical, inaccurate, self-defeating, and unrealistic qualities. Because of the irrational quality of these types of thoughts, they are also referred to as cognitive distortions. This type of self-talk involves excessive concerns and often inaccurate perceptions of reality. This thinking tends to make us feel defeated and afraid. For example:

My back hurts. The cancer has spread! The doctors won't be able to help me this time.

Rationalized Self-Talk

These thoughts are used to deny concern or convince ourselves that everything is okay. This type of self-talk involves an inaccurate perception of reality. For example:

My back hurts. It's nothing. It will go away if I ignore it.

Rational (Balanced) Self-Talk

This type of thinking is reasonable, self-enhancing, accurate, and realistic. The inner dialogue is characterized by appropriate concern, and an accurate, balanced perception of reality. For example:

My back hurts. I may have pulled a muscle. I'll stop by the doctor and have it checked out.

Emphasize that irrational and rationalized thoughts represent extremes in our way of thinking. Participants should strive toward rational, balanced thoughts.

Identifying Self-Talk (10 minutes)

Present the following scenario and examples of self-statements to the group. Have them identify each statement as irrational, rational, or rationalized.

Scenario: *You have been home for a week since your surgery but you are still feeling tired and weak. The yard is a mess, the dog needs to be walked, and the car needs an oil change. The following thoughts go through your head:*

1. *My family/friends are worthless. They are never there when I need them.*

   Type of Self-Talk: Irrational

2. *It's been a week. I should have enough energy by now! I'm probably just using my surgery as an excuse not to do things.*

   Type of Self-Talk: Rationalized

3. *I'll just ignore everything. The lawn can just grow out of control.*

   Type of Self-Talk: Rationalized

4. *I will let my family/friends know how they can help me. Jim can mow the lawn and Ann can take the car in for an oil change. The yard doesn't always have to be spotless. Each person can contribute a little bit, and a thorough cleaning can wait a few more days.*

   Type of Self-Talk: Rational

Role-Play Exercise (5 minutes)

Use examples from last week's homework and have group members role-play irrational, rational, and rationalized responses to situations.

Or, alternatively, present each of the following situations and have participants suggest possible responses. Use the possible responses listed here as examples.

Scenario 1: *You loaned a friend $100 two months ago. Payment was due a month ago, and you would like the money paid back since you now need it.*

Possible Responses:

Irrational: *My friend lied and manipulated me!*

Rationalized: *I can do without the money. He needs it more than I do. I'll just forget it.*

Rational: *My friend may be having further monetary difficulties and may be too embarrassed to call me. I will call him and try to work out a payment agreement.*

Scenario 2: *Your "supervisee" at work regularly misses deadlines.*

Possible Responses:

Irrational: *He is doing this to make me look bad!*

Rationalized: *Someone else can worry about it. I'm busy enough.*

Rational: *He seems to be having a difficult time. Let me see how he needs help.*

Replacing Negative Thoughts with More Rational Responses (10 minutes)

Explain to group members that since inaccurate negative self-talk leads to unnecessary distress and negative emotions, they need to learn to replace negative thinking with more rational thoughts. One of the easiest ways to come up with thought replacements is to target a specific negative thought, identify the type of thought involved, and then generate alternative thoughts. You can use the previously used metaphors (see session 2) to introduce the process of coming up with alternative responses:

As we mentioned before, the appraisal process is very fast (automatic) and, as in the case of learning to drive or improving our swimming style, we must break down the process into steps. By "videotaping" our thought process we can look at it frame by frame, and become more AWARE of the steps involved. Then we can use these same steps to MODIFY our automatic self-talk.

Refer to Figure 7.2 (this diagram is also found in the participant workbook) to demonstrate the place of cognitive restructuring.

Steps to Thought Replacement

Present the following steps to thought replacement. (Adapted from Burns, 1981). You may want to use the phrase "It's as easy as A-B-C-D-E."

Step 1. AWARENESS—Identify Self-Talk
   1. Recognize self-talk (write it down). Separate thoughts about:
       ■ yourself
       ■ the other person
       ■ the situation
   2. Appraise self-talk (irrational, rational, and rationalized). Identify inaccurate or distorted thoughts.
   3. Identify emotions, behaviors, and physical reactions related to self-talk.
   4. Evaluate the intensity of your feelings (low, moderate, high).

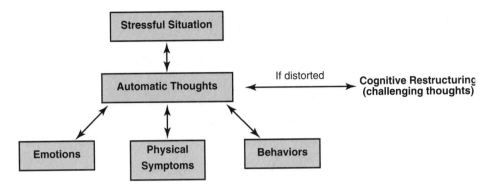

Figure 7.2

Place of Cognitive Restructuring

Step 2. BELIEFS—Rate Degree of Belief in Self-Talk

Rate from 0–100% the degree of belief in each self-talk statement.
Examples:

- ■ "I believe this thought, cognition, or belief is true 95% of the time."
- ■ "I believe this thought is true about half the time (50%)."
- ■ "I don't believe this thought at all (0%)!"

Step 3. CHALLENGE—Question the Self-Talk

Use the following questions to challenge the self-talk statement:

- ■ "Is there any rational support for this idea?"
- ■ "What evidence exists for the falseness of this idea?"
- ■ "What might be the consequences of this situation?"
- ■ "What are the consequences of thinking this way?"
- ■ "What is the worst that could happen to me?"
- ■ "What good things might occur?"

Step 4. DELETE the Inaccurate Negative Self-Talk Statement and Replace It with a More Rational Response

The following questions may help identify more rational responses:

- ■ "What can I say to myself that will reduce excessive negative feelings?"

- "What can I say to myself that will be self-enhancing instead of self-deprecating?"
- "What can I say to myself that will help me appropriately cope with the situation?"
- "How can I restate this situation in new terms?"
- "How would I like to act and feel in the situation? What can I say to myself to help me do this?"

Step 5. EVALUATE How You Feel After the Change

Use the following questions to evaluate the outcome of replacing the inaccurate negative self-talk with more rational responses.
- "Is there a reduction in stress (or an anticipated reduction)?"
- "Is the situation more manageable?"
- "Do I feel better emotionally and/or physically?"

Thought Replacement Exercise (10 minutes)

Have participants look at scenario 1 from the role-play exercise again (*You loaned a friend $100 two months ago. Payment was due a month ago, and you would like the money paid back since you now need it*). Have the group apply steps A-B-C-D-E as previously outlined.

When the group reaches step 4 (Delete and Replace), offer the following strategies and examples:

- Reduce negative thoughts with more rational responses:
  It's reasonable to inquire about the situation.
  He may be angry, but I can live with that.

- Use self-enhancing statements:
  I'll feel better if I know what's going on.

- Facilitate coping with self-talk:
  I'm taking care of myself when I check this out and try to resolve it.

- Think about how you would like to act and feel:
  I'd like to do this in a straightforward way, so I know what to expect.
  I'll feel better knowing I've attempted to resolve the situation.

Further Cognitive Restructuring Practice

Use an example from the group and go through the first four steps again. Have group members help generate alternative thoughts. If group members have difficulty coming up with an example of an overwhelming situation, suggest the experience of having cancer. Break the situation down into manageable pieces, such as treatment, sexuality, and disabilities. Focus on dealing with one aspect at a time.

Helpful Guidelines for Generating Rational Responses (5 minutes)

Review the following guidelines with the group. These will help them generate rational responses.

- Pick specific thoughts to refute and replace.

- Deal with specific problems—not with complicated situations or philosophical stances.

- If you get stuck and can't think of a rational response:

  Come back to it.

  Think of how someone else would respond.

  Think of how you would respond to someone else in the same situation.

- Ask other people how they would respond.

- Identify black-and-white words such as "always," "never," "should," or "can't."

- Learn to describe events in less extreme terms—things can be "inconvenient," "disappointing," "frustrating," or "well-done," as opposed to "terrible," "horrible," "catastrophic," or "perfect."

Examples of Rational Responses

If group members are finding it difficult to generate rational responses, the examples below can be used as an initial response to inaccurate self-talk. These responses can be expanded on with additional rational thoughts appropriate for the particular situation.

- *I may feel negative emotions, but the situation itself doesn't do anything to me.*

- *Nobody's perfect.*

- *Many symptoms are temporary.*

- *We can influence how we feel by the way we think.*

- *Open communication is the key to understanding each other.*

Cognitive Restructuring in Progress

End the discussion by presenting Figure 5.3 (a copy is found in the participant workbook). Emphasize the importance of breaking down overwhelming situations into more manageable pieces.

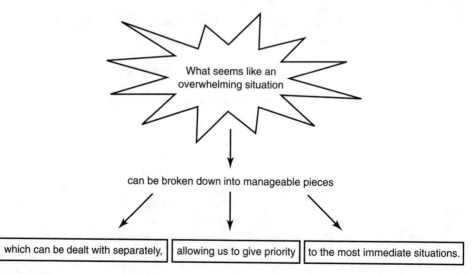

Figure 7.3
Cognitive Restructuring in Progress

Homework (5 minutes)

✎ Have group members review session 5 of the workbook and complete the exercises.

✎ Have group members complete the Cognitive Restructuring Monitoring Sheet for two separate stressful situations. If you'd like to provide group members with additional copies, you may photocopy this sheet from the workbook.

Session Evaluation (5 minutes) (optional)

Have group members complete the session evaluation sheet (see appendix).

| Chapter 8 | *Session 6: Autogenic Training / Coping I* |

(Corresponds to session 6 of the workbook)

Materials Needed

- Flip chart or board

- Copy of participant workbook

- Comfortable chairs for relaxation training

- Copies of relaxation tapes (optional)

- Copies of monitoring sheets (optional)

- Copies of session evaluation sheet (optional)

RELAXATION TRAINING: *Autogenic Training*

Outline

- Discuss adherence to relaxation practice (5 minutes)

- Introduce autogenic training (10 minutes)

- Conduct autogenic exercises for heaviness and warmth (10 minutes)

- Discuss relaxation practice (3 minutes)

- Assign homework (2 minutes)

Discussion of Adherence to Relaxation Practice (5 minutes)

Discuss obstacles or difficulties with relaxation practice. Ask the following questions:

- "What are some of the obstacles you are encountering when trying to conduct a relaxation exercise?"

- "Have any other members experienced these obstacles?"

- "How have you coped with these barriers? Have you been successful?"

- "Is there anything you can do differently (e.g., change environment/location, plan ahead, enlist a friend or spouse to join you in the exercises) to help you carry out these relaxation exercises?"

Optional: collect Relaxation Monitoring Sheets and distribute relaxation tapes.

Introduction to Autogenic Training (10 minutes)

Explain to the group that autogenic training (AT) is a systematic program to teach the body and mind to respond quickly and effectively to verbal commands to relax. It is one of the most effective means for reducing physical tension as well as anxiety.

Background

In the 1880s, Oskar Vogt, a brain psychologist at the Berlin Institute, taught some of his experienced hypnotic subjects to put themselves in a trance. This trance resulted in reduced fatigue and tension, usually accompanied by a feeling of warmth and heaviness. This research influenced Johannes H. Schultz, a German psychiatrist who developed AT in the first half of the twentieth century. Autogenic training uses verbal formulas to achieve a deep state of self-induced relaxation. For example, self-suggestions for warmth and heaviness enable the mind to create these relaxing sensations in the body.

Standard Exercises

Review the two standard exercises to be used with the group. Each exercise will introduce a verbal formula for participants to keep in mind constantly while passively concentrating on a particular part of the body. Participants should repeat the formula to themselves slowly three times, taking about 5 seconds per repetition and pausing about 3 seconds between repetitions.

The first standard exercise involves the theme of heaviness. It promotes relaxation of the muscles in the arms and legs with the phrase "My _____ is heavy." The second standard exercise increases blood flow to the extremities by focusing on warmth. For example, with the phrase "My right hand is warm," more blood begins to flow into the hand and warms it. These themes help counteract the "fight-or-flight" reaction to stress.

Importance of Passive Concentration

Emphasize to group members that in doing these exercises, it is essential that they maintain an attitude of passive concentration. Use the following dialogue to explain what this attitude involves:

You can't force yourself to feel heavy or warm. Instead, you have to let go into the sense of relaxation and allow yourself to experience whatever happens without any expectations. Try to be very aware of your response to the exercise without judging it.

Use passive concentration, which is like what we use when we watch a movie. This is different than the active concentration we use for goal-oriented activities, like playing a game or driving a car. Passive concentration requires you to just notice your experience without analyzing it. Unlike meditation, which we'll be doing in a few weeks, autogenics concentrates on physical sensations rather than mental states.

General Tips for Practice

Also review the following tips for autogenic practice with the group:

- Choose a quiet room. Keep noise and interruptions to a minimum.

- Keep the room at a warm but comfortable temperature.

- Adjust the lighting to a low level.

- Clothing should be loose and comfortable.

- Do these exercises before meals rather than after eating (e.g., in the morning before breakfast).

- Begin by relaxing the body and closing the eyes.

Also stress to participants that when they first attempt autogenics, they should try to reduce all outside distractions. Once they have become more adept, they may be able to practice in an ordinary setting without preparation. You may want to use the following dialogue:

> *When you've become more skilled, autogenics can be practiced for a few minutes during breaks in your regular activities. For example, instead of taking a coffee break at work, take 10 minutes and relax with autogenics. You will not be able to stay completely focused at first. It's okay if your mind wanders. When you find this happening, just immediately return to the repetition of the formula.*

Imagery Suggestions

Today's session will practice two themes: heaviness and warmth. If participants have difficulty achieving a sensation of heaviness or warmth using the verbal formulas, they may want to add visual imagery. For example, they might imagine weights attached to their arms and legs gently pulling them down. Or they might imagine their arms lying on a warm heating pad. Participants should select one imagery prompt that works for them and stay with it throughout the exercise.

Use the following script to conduct the autogenic exercises for heaviness and warmth.

Get into a comfortable position. Close your eyes. Inhale and exhale slowly and deeply. Let go of the events of the day and allow your mind to empty. If thoughts or feelings come up, just notice them and let them pass by as if you were watching them on a movie screen.

Begin by saying to yourself, "I am completely relaxed and at peace." Repeat this phrase slowly three times while breathing deeply, releasing tension with every exhale.

Focus on your right arm and feel it becoming heavy. Say to yourself three times, "My right arm is heavy." Pause between each repetition of the phrase and concentrate on the feeling of heaviness. Then move your attention to your left arm and say to yourself three times, "My left arm is heavy." Feel your arm becoming heavier with each repetition of the phrase. Concentrate on the heaviness in both your arms and say to yourself three times, "Both of my arms are heavy." Breathe deeply and feel yourself becoming more relaxed with every exhale.

Repeat the preceding instructions, substituting legs for arms. Then continue with the following:

Now feel the heaviness in both your arms and legs. Say to yourself three times, "My arms and legs are heavy." Continue to breathe slowly and deeply. Turn your attention to your neck and shoulders; say to yourself three times, "My neck and shoulders are heavy." Feel yourself becoming heavier and heavier, more and more relaxed with each exhale of the breath.

Repeat the entire preceding sequence, substituting warmth for heaviness.

After completing the sequence for both heaviness and warmth, end the exercise with:

Now rest for a few minutes as you gradually become more alert. Say to yourself three times, "I am relaxed and alert." Inhale deeply and exhale, letting go of any remaining tension. When you are ready, slowly open your eyes.

Post-Relaxation Discussion Questions (3 minutes)

- "How did these new exercises feel?"

- "Were you able to feel the warmth and heaviness?"

- "Did they have a relaxing effect on your body?"

Homework (2 minutes)

✎ Have group members practice autogenic exercises for warmth and heaviness at least once a day. They should record stress levels before and after each practice on the Relaxation Monitoring Sheet.

STRESS MANAGEMENT: *Coping I*

Outline

- Check in with group members (5 minutes)

- Review material and homework from previous session (5 minutes)

- Define coping (10 minutes)

- Discuss controllable versus uncontrollable aspects of a situation (5 minutes)

- Discuss problem-focused versus emotion-focused coping (5 minutes)

- Discuss the importance of a fit between the controllability of a stressor and the coping strategy (5 minutes)

- Discuss active versus passive approaches to coping (5 minutes)

- Conduct coping exercise (5 minutes)

- Review the coping process (5 minutes)

- Help group members identify their personal coping styles
  (10 minutes)

- Review steps for matching coping responses to the situation
  (5 minutes)

- Review coping's place in the stress management model (5 minutes)

- Assign homework (5 minutes)

- Have group members complete session evaluation sheet (5 minutes)
  (optional)

Pre-Didactic Check-In (5 minutes)

Go around the room and have each group member share how he is doing and update other group members on any personal news.

Previous Material and Homework Review (5 minutes)

Briefly review the five steps (A-B-C-D-E) to thought replacement presented in the last session.

Review assigned stress management homework (e.g., Cognitive Restructuring Monitoring Sheet). Problem-solve any difficulties group members had completing the homework.

Definition of Coping (10 minutes)

Explain to the group that the term "coping" may have many different meanings for different people. A person's definition of coping is most likely related to his past experiences with different stressful situations. Some people use the word "coping" to convey a negative experience – for example, "I just coped with it." Statements like this one imply that the person could not do anything about the situation but "cope" with it; the person could not affect the outcome. Others have a more optimistic definition of coping – for example, "The situation is bad, but fortunately, I am able to cope with it." This statement conveys a sense of mastery over a difficult situation; the person was able to manage.

Tell participants that this program focuses on the definition of coping that refers to an individual's efforts to manage demands that are appraised as *exceeding his resources* (Lazarus & Folkman, 1984). This means that the person feels unable to do what may be required to deal with a given situation. To build on what has been discussed before, go over the following sequence of events with the group:

1. An event occurs.

2. You have thoughts about it, or appraise the situation.

3. You feel some sort of emotion about the situation.

4. You try to determine how you will respond, or how you will cope, with the unique demands of the situation.

5. Once you've determined a course of action, you initiate the coping response.

Emphasize that coping responses may take many forms, and you are going to talk about some of them shortly. Say that although this may be the first time the group is actually discussing coping in these terms, this is not the first time coping has been introduced in these sessions. In fact, increased awareness of stress patterns, learning relaxation skills, and altering inaccurate or distorted cognitions are all coping strategies. In this session, however, the group will look at coping itself in a slightly different way. They will learn how coping can be broken down into several different categories.

One of the easiest ways to explain the different dimensions of coping is to use a grid to demonstrate how the different dimensions relate to each other. As you go, label the categories on the grid, and once you have finished discussing the aspects of coping, return to the grid to fill it in with examples of coping strategies from the group (see Coping Exercise on p. 117).

Remind the group of the definition of coping as a person's efforts to manage demands that are *appraised* as exceeding resources. The coping response is what a person does after appraising the stressful situation. In-

Table 8.1 Examples of Controllable and Uncontrollable Aspects of Situations

Situation 1: A hurricane warning is issued.

Controllable	Uncontrollable
→ Find a way to protect house/valuables	→ The path of the hurricane
→ Decide whether to evacuate	→ Reactions of other people
→ Stock up on supplies (food, water)	
→ Manage your stressful feelings	

Situation 2: You are diagnosed with prostate cancer.

Controllable	Uncontrollable
→ Choose the right doctor	→ The fact that I have cancer
→ Decide on procedure (if it's an option)	→ Time spent waiting for PSA results

dividual differences in coping actions and resources play a substantial role in affecting how much stress affects a person.

Controllable Versus Uncontrollable Aspects of a Situation (5 minutes)

An important element of the appraisal process involves determining what aspects of the immediate stressor are controllable and what aspects are uncontrollable. Explain that making this distinction is important because it helps us approach a situation in a more effective way. Most situations have both controllable and uncontrollable aspects. Use the examples in Table 8.1 to demonstrate.

Problem-Focused Versus Emotion-Focused Coping (5 minutes)

One way to look at coping is by considering *how* a person might cope with a stressful situation. Explain that coping mechanisms can be identified as problem-focused or emotion-focused activities.

Problem-Focused Coping

Problem-focused coping involves changing a problem or an aspect of a problem that is causing distress by using coping strategies such as:

- cognitive problem solving

- decision making

- conflict resolution

- seeking information

- seeking advice

- goal setting

Give examples of problem-focused coping such as the following:

Problem: *The insurance company is refusing to pay my hospital bills from my prostatectomy surgery.*

Problem-focused coping: *I will send letters to the company, make phone calls to appropriate people, and try to resolve the situation.*

Emotion-Focused Coping

Emotion-focused coping involves regulating the emotional response produced by a stressful situation by using coping strategies such as:

- cognitive reappraisal and reframing

- emotional expression

- behavioral changes (e.g., engaging in pleasant activities)

- physical stress reduction (e.g., exercising, relaxation, deep breathing)

Give examples of emotion-focused coping such as the following:

Problem: *My wife is having a hard time dealing with the changes that have resulted from the surgery.*

Emotion-focused coping: *I will make some time to sit down and talk with her to make sure she's okay, and listen to her concerns. I'll share my experiences with her, and maybe this can bring us closer.*

Fit Between Controllability of the Stressor and Coping Strategy (5 minutes)

According to Folkman et al. (1991), a key to adaptive coping involves making sure there is a fit between the appraisal of the controllability of the stressor and the type of coping process. Explain that *changeable* (controllable) aspects of a stressor are best dealt with using *problem-focused* behaviors, whereas *unchangeable* (uncontrollable) aspects of a stressor may be best dealt with by using *emotion-focused* coping strategies. A poor fit between the appraisal of the stressful situation and the coping behaviors employed may decrease one's possibility of effectively managing the stress and may increase distress. For example, by concentrating problem-focused efforts on a situation that is uncontrollable, a person remains invested in a frustrating situation, which could lead to distress and fatigue.

Remind the group that most situations have both controllable and uncontrollable aspects. Thus, we often use both problem- and emotion-focused strategies in the course of coping with a stressful situation. In addition, the appropriate use of one type of strategy can facilitate the use of the other. For example:

> *Before a doctor's visit, many people feel anxious and concerned about upcoming tests and monitoring. Practicing relaxation exercises can help decrease feelings of anxiety (emotion-focused coping). This reduction in anxiety may help you focus better on information presented by the doctor. This, in turn, will allow you to better use the information provided (problem-focused coping).*

Similarly, patients can choose coping strategies that will contribute to their emotional and physical well-being during the doctor's visit. Rather than catastrophizing, they can break it down into manageable parts and cope with each situation as it arises. Emphasize to the group that, most importantly, the coping response is that part of the stress response that is the easiest to observe and ultimately change.

Active Versus Passive Approaches (5 minutes)

Another dimension of coping involves whether the coping strategy is *actively or directly* approaching the problem or reaction to the problem or whether the coping strategy is *passively or indirectly* dealing with the problem. Explain that this active/passive dimension can be applied to both problem-focused and emotion-focused strategies.

Active Coping Strategies

Active coping strategies are activities that are directly focused on resolving either the problem itself or the emotional consequences of the problem. In other words, active refers to coping that *directly* deals with aspects of the situation. See Table 8.2 for examples.

Passive Coping Strategies

Passive Problem-Focused Strategies tend to involve what we refer to as *behavioral avoidance* and *cognitive avoidance.* These behaviors indirectly approach (or avoid) the problem.

■ BEHAVIORAL AVOIDANCE: The great lengths that people will go to in order to reroute their lives away from an uncomfortable person, place, or activity.

Table 8.2 Examples of Active Coping Strategies

Problem-Focused (for controllable aspects)	Emotion-Focused (for uncontrollable aspects)
Information seeking	Reappraisal of thoughts
Decision making	Reframing thoughts
Conflict resolution	Recognizing and accepting negative emotions
Goal setting/prioritizing	Seeking emotional support/help
Requesting help (activities)	Exercise, massage
Focused activity (alter the situation when possible)	Relaxation exercises, meditation

- COGNITIVE AVOIDANCE: Often takes the form of distraction from or outright denial of the problem at hand; does little to change the nature of the burden.

Passive Emotion-Focused Strategies are indirect actions that tend to focus on decreasing the emotional consequences of stressful situations. Passive strategies often feel good in the short run. In the long run, they are generally ineffective and, in the extreme, may be harmful. Examples of passive emotion-focused behaviors are:

- Feeling helpless or giving up

- Procrastinating

- Stuffing your feelings inside or bottling up your emotions

- Increased consummatory activities such as smoking, eating, alcohol consumption and recreational drug use/abuse. (These activities may serve, at the physical level, to distract or numb one from feelings of anxiety.)

For example, after receiving a diagnosis of cancer, an individual may feel that "this is not happening." To deny the existence of the problem will reduce distress in the short term, but in the long term, will keep him from seeking proper medical treatment and endanger his life. There is also evidence that such indirect actions may actually increase depressed feelings and impair physiological systems such as the immune system (Antoni, M.H., 2003). A growing body of literature has related an attitude of "giving up" or "hopelessness" to a poorer prognosis and shorter survival time for people with some types of cancer.

Coping Exercise (5 minutes)

Draw a grid on the board. Have the group generate a scenario and a list of responses to that stressor. Have group members assign each response to the correct area of the grid. See Table 8.3 for examples.

Table 8.3 Examples of Coping Strategies

Coping Strategy	Problem-focused (for controllable aspects)	Emotion-focused (for uncontrollable aspects)

Active (direct)	Information seeking
	Goal setting
	Decision making
	Conflict resolution
		Reappraisal of situation
		Reframing thoughts
		Pleasant/healthy distractions:
		  Exercise (e.g., walking)
		  Massage
		Accept negative emotions:
		  Acceptance
		  Talk with friends

Passive (indirect)	Behavioral avoidance
	Cognitive avoidance:
	  Denial
	  Not thinking about it
		Smoking, eating, alcohol use
		Not caring for yourself:
		  Don't take medication
		  Miss doctor's appt.
		Stuffing feelings

Coping Process (5 minutes)

Review with the group how when a stressful event occurs, first we have awareness of the event and our reactions to it; next we appraise our thoughts and replace them with more rational responses if needed; then we make appraisals about the controllability of the event and evaluate what resources we have to deal with individual aspects of the situation; finally, we initiate coping efforts to deal with the event. Refer to Figure 8.1 (also found in the workbook).

Identifying Personal Coping Styles (10 minutes)

Ask group members the following questions to help them identify their own personal coping styles.

■ "What are your most common coping strategies?"

■ "Are you more problem-focused or emotion-focused?" (We tend to favor one or the other.)

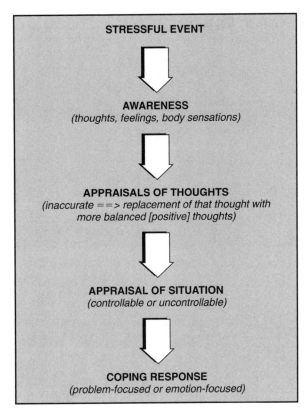

Figure 8.1
Coping Process

- "When do you use active strategies?"

- "Under what circumstances do you use passive strategies?"

Have participants identify their coping responses to situations related to prostate cancer. Discuss the effectiveness of these strategies and what alternative coping responses could be employed.

- "Which strategies were used?"

- "Which were more helpful?"

- "Which were less helpful?"

- "What changes would be beneficial at this point?"

Steps for Matching Coping Responses to the Situation (5 minutes)

Emphasize the importance of matching coping responses to the situation. Review the following steps with the group.

Step 1) Recognize the situation and the related cognitive, emotional, and physical reactions.

Step 2) Break the situation into controllable and uncontrollable aspects. Note: There may be several of each, especially in more complex situations.

Step 3) Generate potential coping strategies for each aspect (problem-focused for controllable aspects; emotion-focused for uncontrollable aspects). Be sure they are active strategies.

Step 4) Set goals and priorities for each aspect of the situation.

Step 5) Choose appropriate coping strategies for each aspect of the situation.

Coping and the Stress Management Model (5 minutes)

Refer to Figure 8.2 (this diagram is also found in the workbook) to review the place of coping in the stress management model.

Facilitator Note

■ *This ends the first part of the program. The next part moves on to anger management, assertive communication, and social support.* ■

Homework (5 minutes)

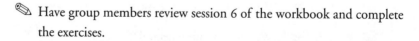 Have group members review session 6 of the workbook and complete the exercises.

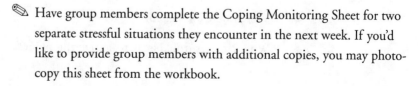 Have group members complete the Coping Monitoring Sheet for two separate stressful situations they encounter in the next week. If you'd like to provide group members with additional copies, you may photocopy this sheet from the workbook.

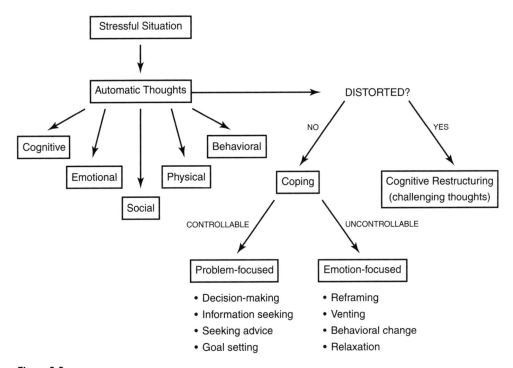

Figure 8.2
Coping and the Stress Management Model

Session Evaluation (5 minutes) (optional)

Have group members complete the session evaluation sheet (see appendix).

Chapter 9

Session 7: Autogenics with Visual Imagery and Positive Self-Suggestions / Coping II

(Corresponds to session 7 of the workbook)

Materials Needed

- Autogenic script from session 6
- Flip chart or board
- Copy of participant workbook
- Comfortable chairs for relaxation training
- Copies of relaxation tapes (optional)
- Copies of monitoring sheets (optional)
- Copies of session evaluation sheet (optional)

RELAXATION TRAINING: *Autogenics with Visual Imagery and Positive Self-Suggestions*

Outline

- Discuss adherence to relaxation practice (5 minutes)
- Introduce autogenics with visual imagery and positive self-suggestions (5 minutes)
- Conduct autogenic exercises (10 minutes)
- Conduct visual imagery and positive self-suggestions exercise (10 minutes)

- Discuss relaxation practice (3 minutes)

- Assign homework (2 minutes)

Discussion of Adherence to Relaxation Practice (5 minutes)

Discuss obstacles or difficulties with relaxation practice. Ask the following questions:

- "What are some of the obstacles you are encountering when trying to conduct a relaxation exercise?"

- "Have any other members experienced these obstacles?"

- "How have you coped with these barriers? Have you been successful?"

- "Is there anything you can do different (e.g., change environment/location, plan ahead, enlist a friend or spouse to join you in the exercises) to help you carry out these relaxation exercises?"

Optional: collect Relaxation Monitoring Sheets and distribute relaxation tapes.

Introduction to Autogenics with Visual Imagery and Positive Self-Suggestions (5 minutes)

This session's autogenic practice incorporates visual imagery and positive self-suggestions. Using visual imagery can enhance the relaxation experience by creating a sense of going on an inner journey. Since participants' attention is turned inward, distractions and other external stimuli may be less noticeable.

Explain that today's exercise aims to put participants in a receptive state of mind where they can suggest to themselves the changes they seek. They can tailor this relaxation to their specific needs such as stress reduction, healing, improving self-esteem, dealing with phobias, or any situation they wish to address. Use the following example to illustrate positive self-suggestions to the group:

For example, if you want to stop smoking, you could introduce a repeated suggestion such as, "I can do without smoking," or "I enjoy breathing pure air."

Note that such deliberate suggestions should be brief and to the point, as well as believable. General suggestions for centering and increasing the depth of relaxation can also be used, such as "I feel a deep sense of calm," or "My mind is quiet; I feel serene and still."

Autogenic Exercises (10 minutes)

This session combines autogenics with visual imagery and positive self-suggestions. Use the script from session 6 to repeat the autogenic exercises for heaviness and warmth.

Visual Imagery and Positive Self-Suggestions Exercise (10 minutes)

From the autogenic exercise move directly into the following imagery script (Adapted from Mason, 1985). This basic script can be expanded with additional imagery as time allows. Tell group members that, as with any imagery exercise, to feel free if necessary to alter the imagery suggestions to ones that they may find to be more useful or comfortable to work with.

Breathe deeply, releasing tension with every exhalation. Let your thoughts float up and out of your mind. Do not hold onto your thoughts, just let them pass on by. As your mind becomes clear, you become calm and relaxed.

Imagine yourself moving further and further down into relaxation. As you reach the depth of your relaxation, you find yourself surrounded by a calm, peaceful scene. Step into this scene and follow a path to a special place of your own choosing. This may be a place that you have been, or that you would like to go, or that only exists in your imagination.

Pick a comfortable spot and lie down, letting your body sink into the ground. Feel a sense of calm and relaxation. The sun gently shines down on you and warms your hands, your feet, your arms and legs. As the warmth spreads over your body, you feel the tension melting away. You drift deeper into a state of calm and relaxation. Your arms and legs become heavier and heavier, and you sink further into the ground. Enjoy the still-ness of your special place.

As you lie comfortable and relaxed, repeat your special phrase to yourself three times. Or say to yourself, "My mind is peaceful. I feel calm and still. My thoughts are turned inward and I am at ease."

Take this feeling of calm and relaxation with you into your day. As you continue to practice this exercise, you will be able to relax more quickly, more deeply.

Now rest for a few minutes as you gradually become more alert. Say to yourself three times, "I am relaxed and alert." Inhale deeply and exhale, letting go of any remaining tension. When you are ready, slowly open your eyes.

Post-Relaxation Discussion Questions (3 minutes)

- "Was it easier to feel heaviness and warmth this week?"

- "Did you find that imagery deepened your relaxation?

- "How do you feel about using positive self-suggestions?"

Homework (2 minutes)

Have group members practice autogenics with visual imagery and positive self-suggestions at least once a day. They should record stress levels before and after each practice on the Relaxation Monitoring Sheet.

STRESS MANAGEMENT: *Coping II*

Outline

- Check in with group members (5 minutes)

- Review material and homework from previous session (15 minutes)

- Recite Serenity Prayer (5 minutes)

- Introduce the concept of acceptance/softening (5 minutes)

- Conduct softening exercise (10 minutes)

- Review coping's place in the stress management model (10 minutes)

- Discuss coping exercise for controllable and uncontrollable aspects (10 minutes)

- Assign homework (5 minutes)

- Have group members complete session evaluation sheet (5 minutes) (optional)

Pre-Didactic Check-In (5 minutes)

Go around the room and have each group member share how he is doing and update other group members on any personal news.

Previous Material and Homework Review (15 minutes)

Facilitator Note

■ *Given the complexity of the "coping" module, a good part of this session is spent reviewing last week's information and using homework examples to work through the process of determining the demands of the situation and then matching coping strategies to those demands.* ■

Review the following points with the group:

- Definition of coping

- Dimensions to coping:

  controllable vs. *uncontrollable* aspects

  problem-focused vs. *emotion-focused* coping

  active vs. *passive* approach

- Coping response

- Chain of events: *stressful event → awareness → appraisal → coping*

- Matching stressors with coping strategies (see Table 8.3 in chapter 8)

- Steps for matching stressors with strategies

After reviewing last session's material, discuss patterns of reactions and patterns of coping using examples from group members' homework (Coping Monitoring Sheet). Use the following questions:

- "What coping patterns do we tend to employ?"

- "Do they match the situation?"

- "What active approaches do we tend to use?"

- "How can we change the passive approaches?"

Serenity Prayer—A Commonly Used Guide to Coping with Adversity (5 minutes)

Explain that one way to understand the importance of determining whether a situation or problem is controllable or uncontrollable is to think of an often-recited prayer. Even if group members are not very religious (or are not religious at all), they have probably heard of (or know about) "The Serenity Prayer." Ask the group if they are familiar with this prayer and have a group member recite it:

God, grant me the serenity to accept the things I cannot change,
the courage to change the things I can
and the wisdom to know the difference.

Introduction to Acceptance/Softening (5 minutes)

Tell the group that sometimes we are confronted with situations that are so distressing or difficult that even after we have done the coping and made the stressor smaller, there is still some emotional distress to be dealt with. An example of this is when we lose someone we care about, either through the end of a relationship or death. The following dialogue can be used:

> *Our natural tendency is to brace against pain. We tighten around physical pain or attempt to block off emotional distress. However, trying to fight or avoid pain only makes it worse. This sets up a negative cycle of pain and resistance. To break this cycle, we can instead soften around the pain. Softening means acknowledging the hurt, letting ourselves experience it, and accepting it with compassion. Often when we process painful feelings in this way, we are surprised at how what before looked totally unmanageable becomes manageable.*

Emphasize that our attitude toward our feelings and our physical pain is important in how much stress we feel. By accepting our feelings and our experiences, we eliminate the stress of bracing against them, or running away from them, and allow ourselves to use as much energy as possible to deal with our life situations directly. We may not like the fact that we are feeling something; but opening up to what is there, without judgment, can often bring a sense of release and relief. This stance is one of self-acceptance, and it allows us to accept what *is* and not what we would *like* it to be. This kind of attitude allows us to take in as much information as possible, deal with the reality of the situation, and maximize our options.

Softening Exercise (10 minutes)

Take the group through the following exercise in softening as a response to painful feelings and emotions:

> *Think about someone you have had trouble with. Or think of something you're not looking forward to. Feel the feeling associated with that situation in your body. Just allow that feeling to be, gently, with-*

out judging it, and without pulling away from it. You might let your-self put your hand over the place that hurts in a way that almost soothes it, and say quietly to yourself, "This is what I feel right now and it is real."

You will find that the feeling may loosen or release somewhat. Let yourself embrace that feeling as you would a hurt child. Acknowledge whatever attitudes, feelings, or thoughts arise into awareness as you continue to pay attention to the sensation, moment to moment. Stay with this feeling for a few more moments. Then gently bring your awareness back to the room, keeping with you the awareness toward yourself.

Discuss group members' reactions to the exercise. Encourage practice using physical pain also. To do so, participants should take a deep breath and relax the muscles around the painful area. As they continue breathing, they should allow the painful sensations to occur. The aim is to focus on the pain without tightening around it.

Review of Coping and the Stress Management Model (10 minutes)

Review coping's place in the stress management model as introduced in the last session (Figure 8.2). Refer participants to the copy of the model in session 7 of workbook as you walk them through it.

Coping Exercise for Controllable and Uncontrollable Aspects (10 minutes)

Use the following example to have participants practice matching cop-ing strategies to the controllability of the situation.

Let's say that you go to the doctor for your routine check-up, and he tells you that your PSA is elevated. He explains that this is a sign of recurrence, and that even though the prostate was removed, some stray cancer cells have spread.

Ask the following questions:

■ "What is uncontrollable?"

■ "What is controllable?"

■ "How might you use problem-focused coping to deal with the controllable aspects of recurrence?"

■ "How might you use emotion-focused coping to deal with the uncontrollable aspects of recurrence?"

Homework (5 minutes)

✎ Have group members review session 7 of the workbook and complete the exercises.

✎ Have group members practice the softening technique.

✎ Have group members complete the Matching and Modifying Coping Monitoring Sheet for two separate stressful situations they encounter in the next week. If you'd like to provide group members with additional copies, you may photocopy this sheet from the workbook.

Session Evaluation (5 minutes) (optional)

Have group members complete the session evaluation sheet (see appendix).

Chapter 10 | Session 8: Mantra Meditation / Anger Management

(Corresponds to session 8 of the workbook)

Materials Needed

- Flip chart or board

- Copy of participant workbook

- Comfortable chairs for relaxation training

- Copies of relaxation tapes (optional)

- Copies of monitoring sheets (optional)

- Copies of session evaluation sheet (optional)

RELAXATION TRAINING: _Mantra Meditation_

Outline

- Discuss adherence to relaxation practice (5 minutes)

- Introduce meditation (10 minutes)

- Review instructions for mantra meditation (15 minutes)

- Conduct mantra meditation exercise (10 minutes)

- Discuss meditation practice (5 minutes)

- Assign homework (2 minutes)

Discussion of Adherence to Relaxation Practice (5 minutes)

Discuss obstacles or difficulties with relaxation practice. Ask the following questions:

- "How often did you practice relaxation?"

- "What barriers have you encountered?"

- "Was there anything you could do to overcome these barriers?"

Optional: collect Relaxation Monitoring Sheets and distribute relaxation tapes.

Introduction to Meditation (10 minutes)

Definition of Meditation

Define meditation as the practice of *uncritically* attempting to focus the mind on the "object" of meditation. Objects vary from one tradition to the next and almost anything can be used to center the attention—one's breathing, a candle flame, etc. This session teaches mantra meditation, which involves the repetition of a syllable, word, or group of words.

Quality of Thought

During the course of meditation, it is expected that the mind will wander. The heart of meditation lies in continually refocusing the attention back to the object of meditation. In doing so, meditators may realize how much certain thoughts are possibly interfering with their thinking. However, by being able to refocus on the task at hand, whether it is a meditation exercise or some other task, they may be able to put those intrusive thoughts aside. (That is not to say one would never deal with these thoughts and the events that are leading to them. We learned in the coping sessions how to address stressful situations in an effective manner.)

Benefits of Meditation

In the late 1960s and early 1970s, Dr. Herbert Benson and his colleagues at Harvard Medical School studied volunteer practitioners of Transcendental Meditation (Benson, 1975). Benson and others demonstrated that during meditation:

■ Heart rate and breathing slow down

■ Blood pressure decreases in patients with elevated blood pressure

■ Oxygen consumption decreases by 20 percent

■ Levels of blood lactate (which rise during stress and fatigue) drop

■ Skin conductance decreases (stress induces sweat, which is a good conductor of electrical charges)

■ Alpha brain waves, another sign of relaxation, are increased

Benson went on to show that any meditation practice could duplicate these physiological changes as long as four factors were present:

1. a relatively quiet environment

2. a mental device that provides a constant stimulus

3. a comfortable position

4. practicing approximately 20 minutes or twice daily

Instructions for Mantra Meditation Practice (15 minutes)

Choosing a Mantra

Before beginning meditation practice, have participants select a word or syllable that they enjoy, preferably one that has a healing or spiritual connotation to them. Inform the group that it is often easier to concentrate on a word with more than one syllable, and, each syllable should have the same emphasis. Some like to use the word "one." Many meditators prefer the universal mantra, "Ohm," or "Shalom," which has two syllables.

When practicing alone, it may be easier for participants to repeat the word out loud, as this will provide an additional means to focus.

Difference Between Relaxation and Meditation

Explain that the biggest difference between relaxation and meditation is that, in relaxation, we are looking to dissociate and move away from the stressors, whereas, in meditation, we are looking to relax our bodies so that we can begin to focus. Stress that *alertness* and *awareness* are key in meditation; so, even though participants should be comfortable and well supported, they should not practice meditation in bed or in a recliner, because it is then too easy to let go and fall asleep.

Postures for Meditation

To prepare group members for meditation, go over the following postures (derived from Davis et al., 1988).

Basic Position

Sit in a chair, with your feet flat on the floor, your knees comfortably apart, and your hands resting in your lap.

Back

Your back should be straight (but not rigid). Let your spinal column directly support the weight of your head. Do this by pulling your chin in slightly. Allow the small of your back to arch.

Balance

Rock briefly from side to side, then from front to back to find your balance. Your upper torso should rest securely on your hips.

Mouth

Close your mouth and breathe through your nose. Let your tongue rest on the roof of your mouth.

Hands

Your hands can rest comfortably in your lap or on your knees, or they can rest open on your knees with your forefingers and thumbs touching.

Breathing

During meditation, diaphragmatic breathing is the most relaxing. Allow deep diaphragmatic breaths to center you as you begin to meditate. You should notice that your breath begins to rest low in your belly, rather than in your upper body.

Grounding/Centering Oneself in a Meditative Position

In addition to reviewing meditative postures with the group, emphasize the importance of grounding or centering oneself in a meditative position. That is, when getting in position to meditate, participants should focus on their current state of being. They should note all of their physical sensations—how they are sitting, how it feels to be in the chair, how their bodies take up space. This will facilitate the transition into a meditative state and help reduce any interference with these exercises.

Meditative Attitude

A passive attitude is essential to meditation. Emphasize to participants that it is natural for other thoughts to break their concentration on the object of meditation. Part of the practice of meditation is learning how to let these thoughts go. When thoughts arise, participants should just let them pass by without judgment and return their attention to their mantras.

Mantra Meditation Exercise (10 minutes)

Before beginning the meditation exercise, you can tell participants that they will start by getting centered in their positions again and taking several deep breaths. They will then move toward focusing on their mantra for about 5 minutes. You will then end the exercise by asking them to take a deep breath and come back feeling refreshed and alert. Use the following script to conduct the meditation (adapted from Mason, 1985):

Get into your meditative position. Take several deep breaths and allow all of the day's activities and concerns to fall away. Do not hold on to any of them. Just let them pass without allowing them to bother you. Begin to focus on your breath, breathing slowly and naturally. Breathe away any thoughts that may be distracting or disturbing you. As your mind becomes clear, you may start to feel calm and relaxed.

Take a moment to scan your body and become aware of any held tension. Focus and release tension in your feet . . . your legs . . . your abdomen . . . your chest . . . your hands . . . your arms . . . your shoulders . . . your neck . . . and your head. Let go of any tension remaining in any part of your body. Now shift your attention back to your breath, which has established its own regular and even pattern.

Begin to repeat your mantra over and over. Let your mantra find its own rhythm; do not force it. Focus on your mantra with minimal effort. Whenever your mind wanders, gently bring it back to your mantra. If you observe any sensations in your body, just notice them, and then return to the repetition of your mantra. If you have any distracting thoughts, just notice them, and then bring your attention back to your mantra.

Maintain soft awareness of each repetition of your mantra. Remain in this state as long as you want, repeating your mantra at regular intervals until you are completely calm and relaxed. When you are ready to end your meditation, take a deep breath, exhale fully, and open your eyes. You can say to yourself, "I am refreshed and alert."

Discussion of Meditation (5 minutes)

Use the following questions to begin the group discussion:

■ "How did you find this experience?"

- "What sort of distractions did you experience?"

- "Was there any turning point at which the exercise became easier?"

Emphasize that distractions are the rule, not the exception. These distractions may range from verbal thoughts to visual imaginings. The important thing is not to hold on to them and analyze them during meditation. If particular thoughts or images keep recurring, participants might want to take a look at these when they are not meditating. Distractions during meditation can sometimes be a clue to what's bothering us.

Also, stress that meditation may not become easier until they have had weeks of practice. Like acquiring any new skill, learning may be gradual but experienced as a sudden turning point. Sometimes the meditator must face the same obstacles at the start of every session. Reassure participants that these are usually overcome within the first few minutes of meditation.

Homework (2 minutes)

✎ Have group members practice mantra meditation at least once a day. They should record stress levels before and after each practice on the Relaxation Monitoring Sheet.

STRESS MANAGEMENT: *Anger Management*

Outline

- Check in with group members (5 minutes)

- Review material and homework from previous session (5 minutes)

- Discuss anger awareness (10 minutes)

- Have group members complete the Self-Evaluation Questionnaire (5 minutes)

- Discuss unhealthy ways to express anger (10 minutes)

- Have group recognize anger behaviors (5 minutes)

- Discuss the importance of awareness of dynamics and other factors (5 minutes)

- Review the consequences of anger (5 minutes)

- Teach how to change maladaptive anger patterns (10 minutes)

- Assign homework (5 minutes)

- Have group members complete session evaluation sheet (5 minutes) (optional)

Pre-Didactic Check-In (5 minutes)

Go around the room and have each group member share how he is doing and update other group members on any personal news.

Previous Material and Homework Review (5 minutes)

Refer to Figure 8.1. in chapter 8 for an overview of the coping process. Review matching coping responses to the demands of the situation (problem-focused for controllable aspects and emotion-focused for uncontrollable aspects). Briefly discuss softening in response to painful feelings.

Review assigned stress management homework (e.g., Matching and Modifying Coping Monitoring Sheet). Problem-solve any difficulties group members had completing the homework.

Increasing Anger Awareness (10 minutes)

Note: portions of this anger management module were adapted from Ironson, Lutgendorf, Starr, & Costello (1989).

Definitions of Anger

Have group members come up with some definitions of anger. One question that may help with the discussion is: "How do you know you're angry?" List possible signs of anger and their categories:

Physical sensations: *tense, shaking, flushed*

Cognition: *blaming, vengeful*

Emotions: *irritation, annoyance, hate*

Behaviors: *outbursts, withdrawal, coldness*

Personal Anger Triggers (What Makes You Angry?)

Have group members come up with things that make them angry and list these on the board. Use the following questions to generate examples:

- "What makes you angry?"

- "What are your personal anger triggers?"

- "Are there any individuals that make you angry?"

- "What kinds of situations cause your anger?"

Examples: *frustration, disappointments, cheating, lying, rudeness, procrastination, carelessness, feeling incompetent, lateness, irresponsibility, harassment, having prostate cancer, inconsideration, side effects of treatment (e.g., urinary incontinence, erectile dysfunction)*

Attitudes Toward Anger

Discuss group members' attitudes toward anger. Ask how they feel about being angry and review possible responses:

- "It is wrong to be angry."

- "It is shameful to be angry."

- "It is allowable to be angry."

- "It is okay to be angry. Anger is a normal human emotion."

Emphasize that anger is an emotion that we all experience and can be healthy when expressed appropriately. The problem is that many people do not feel comfortable expressing mild levels of anger, which usually occur before a situation escalates. Since one does not express anger early on in these situations, the situation can worsen, thus fueling more anger and eventually leading to a state of anger or frustration that can get out of hand (e.g., exploding at someone). However, it is not necessary to let situations escalate. By expressing anger, concern, frustration, and the like in an adaptive way, one can prevent matters from getting worse and eventually avoid a potentially explosive situation.

Patterns of Anger Expression

It is important for participants to increase their understanding of the role that anger plays in their lives. For example, do they go to any extreme to avoid anger? Or do they bottle up their anger until they reach a breaking point and explode at anyone who happens to be there?

Explain that the first step is to recognize that our reactions to anger are learned. Like many of our emotions, we are "taught" when, where, and how to express anger. Much of this training occurs in our families. Just as we learned how to express our anger and to respond to others' anger, we can learn new ways to handle angry feelings.

Self-Evaluation Questionnaire: Developing Anger Awareness (5 minutes)

Have participants turn to the Self-Evaluation Questionnaire in the workbook and work on it for a few minutes. Once they have finished, discuss any insights they have found. Connect past experiences with present behavior patterns. Use the following questions for group discussion:

- "What did you learn about anger?"

- "Has that carried over into your relationships today?"

- "Is anger expression difficult for you?"

- "What happened when you expressed your anger?"

- "What happens when you don't express your feelings?"

- "Do you ever feel out of control with your anger?"

- "Do you think that expressing anger is good or bad?"

Expressing Anger (10 minutes)

Discuss with participants how they express anger. Tell the group that we tend to behave in extremes, either by stifling our anger (i.e., stuffing it down), or "exploding"—verbally, emotionally, and perhaps physically.

Physical Consequences of Explosive Anger

There are physical consequences to explosive anger. Ask the group to generate a list of physical symptoms associated with explosive anger. Add these to the list if not mentioned:

- Increased blood pressure

- Increased blood flow (feeling flushed, red faced)

- Increased heart rate

- Increased muscle tension

Explosive Anger Appraisal

Tell group members that in appraising our angry feelings, we must take our own responses and that of others into consideration. We can then apply the methods we learned to form more balanced thoughts.

Step 1) Examine your appraisal of the situation.

- "What are you saying to yourself?"

- "What is the valid part of your anger?"

- "Are any distorted thoughts contributing to or exacerbating your experience of anger?" (e.g., "No one treats me with respect" or "Everyone steps on me.")

Remind group members to watch out for "black and white thinking" and "should" statements. These often exacerbate anger.

Step 2) Examine the other person's response.

- "Where is the other person coming from?"

- "Is the other person's thinking distorted?"

Stress to group members that it is important to respect the other person's position. People are more likely to listen to us when we consider their vantage point.

Physical Consequences of Stifling or Stuffing Down Anger

Like explosive anger, stifling or stuffing down anger also has physical consequences. Ask participants for physical sensations they have when they stifle their anger. Add the following if not mentioned by the group:

- Increased blood pressure

- Increased heart rate

- Increased muscle tension

- Stomach in a knot

Use the following questions to generate discussion:

- "What happens when you suppress your anger?"

- "Where does all that energy go?"

- "What might that mean for you physically?"

Stifling Anger Appraisal

Have group members begin to look at the process:

- Notice physical symptoms.

- Acknowledge your anger (don't invalidate your emotion).

- Recognize in what situations, or with what people, you tend to deny your anger.

Again, participants will need to appraise their and others' responses to the situation and apply the methods they have learned to form more balanced thoughts. Review the steps and questions listed previously for appraising anger. Substitute examples of distorted thoughts in connection to stifling anger (e.g., "I should not be angry about this" or "I should not make waves.")

Recognizing Anger Behaviors (5 minutes)

Have group members come up with *behaviors* which they use to express (or not express) anger and list them on the board. Separate these into two columns:

Stuffers: rarely express anger or express it indirectly

Exploders: express anger often and at times loudly and unfairly

Add the following examples to the list if not mentioned by the group:

Stuffers	Exploders
ruminating/stewing	yelling
coldness	intimidating
being "extra nice"	nit-picking
backbiting	blaming
silent treatment	throwing things/hitting

Awareness of Dynamics and Other Factors (5 minutes)

Dynamics of Relationships and Situations

Another step to anger management is recognizing one's position of power (e.g., in one's relationship with a boss versus with a colleague who is at an equal or subordinate position within the company). Explain that one's position of power is a consideration when expressing anger. With persons in a position over one, like the boss, the consequences of a confrontation may not be worth the potential benefits.

Another consideration is whether one has a continuing relationship with the person (e.g., "Is this your spouse or a cashier?"). In closer, more long-standing relationships, one may be willing to share deeper expressions of feelings than in casual interactions. The hope is that the person will modify her behavior in the future of the continuing relationship. In a casual interaction the likelihood of ever interacting again with that person is low; hence, the value of sharing personal feelings is likely not worth the investment.

Other Internal and External Factors

Other factors, both internal and external, may contribute to an aggravating situation. Encourage participants to:

■ Recognize *external* factors. Evaluate the extenuating circumstances.

■ Recognize the impact of your current state of mind on your responses. Are you hungry? Have you had enough sleep? Are you sick?

■ Recognize *internal* factors: Know what your "buttons" are. Know what sets you off. Know what issues you are sensitive to!

Consequences of Anger (5 minutes)

Review the consequences of anger with the group by using the following questions and answers.

1. Does anger ever empower you or make things happen for you?
   Anger can help you:
   - stand up for yourself
   - protect others
   - go after things you want

2. Does anger ever disempower you?
   Anger can lead you to:
   - be too upset to work things out
   - withdraw from the situation
   - be embarrassed by your reaction

Changing Maladaptive Anger Patterns (10 minutes)

The following questions can help group members begin to change maladaptive anger patterns:

Questions to ask yourself: ASAP

$A \rightarrow$ ***Awareness:*** *Who or what am I really angry with or about?*

$S \rightarrow$ ***Source:*** *Why am I angry? What is the real cause?*

$A \rightarrow$ ***Alternatives:*** *What do I want to do? Do I have alternatives for accomplishing the same thing?*

$P \rightarrow$ ***Plan:*** *What is my "plan of action"?*

Steps to Changing Anger Patterns

Present the following strategy to the group.

Step 1.   **Recognize you are angry.**
- Note physical symptoms.
- Acknowledge your feelings.

Step 2.   **Decide if you can take action now or should wait until later.**
- Are you too upset to be calm and straightforward?
- Do you need time to think about the situation?
- Does the other person need time to cool off and/or think?

Step 3.   **Assess situation dynamics (i.e., intimate, acquaintance, stranger, work).**
- Power differentials:
  Is this your spouse, your boss, your equal, your employee, or a service person?
  How would this affect your reaction/behavior?
- Relationship factors (i.e., intimate, acquaintance, stranger, work):
  Is this an ongoing relationship or a short-term one?
  How important is this relationship to you?
- Extenuating factors:
  Are there any extenuating circumstances to consider?
  Are you/the other person in a bad mood for an unrelated reason (e.g., hungry, tough day)?
  Are there outside pressures impacting the situation?
- Internal factors:
  Is one of your "buttons" being pushed? (e.g., lateness, sloppiness, disrespect)
  Are you over-reacting?

Step 4.   **Take action.**
- Reappraise.
  What are you telling yourself?
  Do you recognize any cognitive distortions/"shoulds"?
  What is the *automatic reaction* here?

■ Recognize your needs in the situation.

What is it that is not happening?

What is a fair result for you?

■ Recognize the other person's needs.

■ Consider the desired outcome and future relationship.

What is the best possible result?

What would be fair to each person?

■ List your alternatives and pick the best one, even though it may not be the most comfortable one for you.

■ When the timing is right, take action.

Speak your mind.

Change your behavior.

Possible Responses to Consider in an Action Plan

Make group members aware that there are more possibilities than stuffing one's anger or blowing up. Present the following alternatives and encourage participants to start learning which of these works for them.

A → Assertive behavior

• Tell person how you feel

• Ask for what you need

B → Blowing off some steam by talking to someone else

C → Cooling down

D → Defusing (e.g., find an unbiased third-party negotiator)

E → Emotion-focused behavior

• Exercise

• Relaxation

• Support from friends/family

• Express emotions in safe way

F → Focus on any positive aspects of the situation

G → "Let it Go" when appropriate (different from stuffing)

H → Humor (joke, laugh)

I → Information seeking

• Ask for advice

• Search for more information

Homework (5 minutes)

✎ Have group members review session 8 of the workbook and complete the exercises.

✎ Have group members review their answers to the Self-Evaluation Questionnaire.

✎ Have group members complete the Anger Management Monitoring Sheet for two separate stressful events they encounter in the next week. If you'd like to provide group members with additional copies, you may photocopy this sheet from the workbook.

Session Evaluation (5 minutes) (optional)

Have group members complete the session evaluation sheet (see appendix).

Chapter 11 | *Session 9: Mindfulness Meditation / Assertive Communication*

(Corresponds to session 9 of the workbook)

Materials Needed

- Flip chart or board

- Copy of participant workbook

- Comfortable chairs for relaxation training

- Copies of relaxation tapes (optional)

- Copies of monitoring sheets (optional)

- Copies of session evaluation sheet (optional)

RELAXATION TRAINING: *Mindfulness Meditation*

Outline

- Discuss adherence to relaxation practice (5 minutes)

- Introduce mindfulness meditation (5 minutes)

- Conduct mindfulness meditation exercise (20 minutes)

- Discuss meditation practice (3 minutes)

- Assign homework (2 minutes)

Discussion of Adherence to Relaxation Practice (5 minutes)

Discuss obstacles or difficulties with relaxation practice. Ask the following questions:

■ "How often did you practice the relaxation exercise?"

■ "What barriers have you encountered?"

■ "Was there anything you could do to overcome these barriers?"

Optional: collect Relaxation Monitoring Sheets and distribute relaxation tapes.

Introduction to Mindfulness Meditation (5 minutes)

Explain to the group that mindfulness means being fully aware and open to what each moment holds. It is a relaxed state of attentiveness to both the inner world of thoughts and feelings and the outer world of actions and perceptions. You may want to use the following dialogue in your discussion:

> For example, mindfulness when eating means being fully present and enjoying the food rather than thinking about other things. When taking a walk, mindfulness means being open to the sense of movement and to the sights, sounds, and smells around you. It means living your life fully in the moment wherever you are and whatever you're doing. Being mindful means the joy is not in finishing an activity — the joy is in doing it.

Tell group members that today's exercise blends some of the breathing and meditation techniques they have already practiced. However, the focus will be on raising awareness of the sensations they are experiencing at the moment. This practice can help them develop a sense of mindfulness in all their daily activities and their experience of the world around them.

Mindfulness Meditation Exercise (20 minutes)

Use the following script to conduct the meditation (adapted from Kabat-Zinn, 1990). This basic script can be expanded on as time allows.

Get comfortable and begin by breathing deeply. Inhale and exhale, allowing your breath to find its own rhythm. Listen to my voice in the background, but don't concern yourself with how well you are paying attention. Trust your mind to follow the instructions as it needs to.

When you meditate, you turn your awareness to a quiet place within. Mindfulness is the practice of being fully aware of your experience of each moment. As you meditate, you will become mindful of your breath, the sensations in your body, your thoughts and feelings, or whatever rises into your awareness.

To begin meditation, sit with a straight back and head balanced comfortably. Rest your hands in your lap and close your eyes. Take a few deep, cleansing breaths. Begin to turn your attention inward. Use the breath to let go of any tension. (Pause for 15 seconds.)

Become aware of the natural rhythm of your breath as it rises and falls. Some breaths may be long, others short. Your breathing may be smooth or irregular at times. Take notice without judgment, without comment. Just let it be. As you are mindful of each breath, be open to the moment and accepting of whatever it brings. (Pause for 15 seconds.)

As you continue to be aware of your breath, move your focus to any sensations that may be present in your body. Notice how you are sitting, how it feels where your body and chair meet. Let go and feel your body become heavier, more relaxed. Be mindful of any shifts in the body. (Pause for 15 seconds.)

Now focus your awareness on the thoughts in your mind. All kinds of thoughts are continuously arising – worries, fears, hopes, fantasies. This is the mind's natural state. Just watch each thought come and go. Be mindful of the process, simply noticing how thoughts are constantly surfacing, moving, and fading away. At some point you may notice that your awareness has drifted away with the stream of thoughts. Just notice your mind has wandered, without judgment, and gently return your attention to the breath. (Pause for 15 seconds.)

For the next two minutes, keep your breath in the foreground of your awareness while letting any sensations in your body, any thoughts, and anything else you may experience continue in the background. Let the breath ground you in the present moment. (Pause for 2 seconds.)

As you come to end of this meditation, appreciate that you have given this quiet time to yourself. As you practice mindfulness of breath, of sensations, of thoughts, and so on, the benefits of this practice will expand. The time you spend in meditation will help you be more open and aware, more mindful, during the rest of the day. It will help focus your mind and bring a kind of balance to all of your activities. Now, at your own pace, bring your awareness back to the room. When you are ready, open your eyes, feeling refreshed.

Post-Meditation Discussion Questions (3 minutes)

- "How did you find this experience?"

- "What sort of distractions did you experience?"

- "Was there any noticeable difference from last week's meditation experience?"

Homework (2 minutes)

✎ Have group members practice mindfulness meditation at least once a day. They should record stress levels before and after each practice on the Relaxation Monitoring Sheet.

STRESS MANAGEMENT: *Assertive Communication*

Outline

- Check in with group members (5 minutes)

- Review material and homework from previous session (5 minutes)

- Present the four basic interpersonal styles (10 minutes)

- Have group members role-play interpersonal styles (5 minutes)

- Introduce the components of assertive communication (10 minutes)

- Discuss the importance of assertiveness to stress management (5 minutes)

- Discuss common barriers to assertive behavior (5 minutes)

- Have group members role-play assertive responses (5 minutes)

- Review steps to more assertive behavior (5 minutes)

- Assign homework (5 minutes)

- Have group members complete session evaluation sheet (5 minutes) (optional)

Pre-Didactic Check-In (5 minutes)

Go around the room and have each group member share how he is doing and update other group members on any personal news.

Previous Material and Homework Review (5 minutes)

Review anger awareness and anger management techniques from the last session.

Review assigned stress management homework (e.g., Anger Management Monitoring Sheet). Problem-solve any difficulties group members had completing the homework.

Four Basic Interpersonal Styles (10 minutes)

Learning to be assertive can be difficult, especially for those who mistake aggression for assertiveness. It is helpful to start assertiveness training with a presentation of the four basic interpersonal styles. These styles represent patterns which we use to relate and communicate with one another. As we develop our personalities and interpersonal styles, we tend to form these patterns and, without much thought, we engage in them when relating to others. As outlined here, there are advantages and disadvantages to each style. However, some patterns like aggressiveness tend to have more negative consequences, while styles that involve more of an assertive interaction tend to have more positive outcomes. Review each style with the group.

AGGRESSIVENESS: Standing up for what one believes to be one's rights by denying feelings of other people.

(+) **Advantage:** People usually don't push an aggressive person around.

(−) **Disadvantage:** People avoid an aggressive person.

PASSIVENESS: Indirectly violating one's own rights by failing to express honest feelings and beliefs.

(+) **Advantage:** Passive individuals rarely experience direct rejection.

(−) **Disadvantage:** Other people end up making choices for the passive individual, making it hard for the individual to achieve personal goals. Passivity also leads to built-up resentment and guilt for not taking care of oneself.

PASSIVE-AGGRESSIVE: Indirectly and passively resistant, one pretends to go along with another's wishes, but does what one wants to do anyway.

(+) **Advantage:** A passive-aggressive person avoids direct conflict.

(−) **Disadvantage:** Passive-aggressiveness can often cause more interpersonal conflict than directly approaching a situation or person.

ASSERTIVE: Standing up for one's own rights and expressing one's individual feelings or beliefs in a direct way that does not violate the rights of others.

(+) **Advantage:** One can choose one's own goals, not turn people off, promote self-efficacy and self-esteem, and decrease interpersonal conflict.

(−) **Disadvantage:** People who are less comfortable or familiar with the direct expression of feelings and desires may withdraw from, or grow anxious or irritable during an exchange with an assertive person.

Diagram of Interpersonal Styles

Draw the diagram depicted below on board or flip chart. The diagram is a good way to represent the four interpersonal styles on a continuum of disregard/regard for the rights and needs of others and one's own rights and needs. Passive and Aggressive are depicted as two extremes on the continuum and Passive-Aggressive and Assertive are depicted as hybrids which contain the worst and the best aspects of passivity and aggression, respectively. Refer to continuum of anger from explosive (i.e., aggressive) to stifling (i.e., passive).

Interpersonal Style Role-Play Exercise (5 minutes)

Briefly role-play these interpersonal styles in front of the group. Have group members practice identifying different interpersonal styles utiliz-

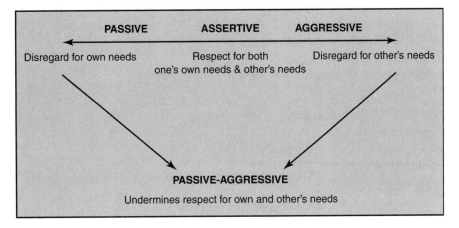

Figure 11.1.
Diagram of Interpersonal Styles

ing the diagram (Fig. 11.1). Note: A copy of this exercise can be found in the participant workbook.

Situation: *You are returning a defective microwave oven during busy store hours. The clerk asks if you dropped it, placed metal objects in it, or if your house had electrical problems.*

Responses:

■ *Complain in a loud voice and exhibit a blaming/accusing attitude.* (Aggressive)

■ *You are intimidated by the clerk, question your rights, and decide to stay with the faulty merchandise.* (Passive)

■ *You appear to take the clerk's remarks quietly, but bad-mouth him to other customers or go to the manager.* (Passive-Aggressive)

■ *You calmly express your wish to exchange the merchandise and stand by your decision.* (Assertive)

Discussion Questions

■ "What behavior helped you identify the interpersonal style?"

■ "Can you think of descriptions for those who exhibit these behaviors?"

■ "How would you feel acting this way?"

Components of Assertive Communication (10 minutes)

Introduce the following components to assertive communication:

1. Sending an assertive message.

2. Listening and responding to the other person's message.

3. Problem-solving conflicts.

Sending an Assertive Message

Language:

- Expresses negative feelings in a non-blaming way

- Points out how others' behaviors concretely affect you while owning your own feelings about the situation

Compare the two examples:

Blaming "You" Message: "When you are late, you make me feel unimportant."

Assertive "I" Message: "When you are late, I often doubt my importance and feel insecure about our friendship."

I want statements (e.g., "I want to eat dinner on time tonight.")

- Clarifies what you really want

- Allows other person to understand how to fulfill your wants

I feel statements: (e.g., "I feel slightly irritated when you don't call to let me know you'll be late.")

- Clarifies how you feel without blaming or attacking the other person

- Should be specific and quantify your feelings (e.g., "I feel *slightly irritated* and concerned") rather than generalizations (e.g., "I feel terrible")

Empathic Assertion: (e.g., "I know that you have a lot of work to get finished and that it is difficult for you to gauge when it will be done but I need you to call if you are going to be late so I can organize my own schedule today.")

- Contains two statements:
  1. The first statement recognizes the other person's situation, feelings, beliefs, and wants.
  2. The second asserts your wants, feelings, and beliefs.

- Communicates sensitivity for the other person without a total disregard for your rights

Warn participants to watch out for conveying *sarcastic messages*. Assertiveness may be misinterpreted as passive-aggressive or sarcastic if speakers don't pay attention to their tone of voice.

Effective Listening

Stress to the group the importance of effective listening. Listening to others often encourages them to listen to us more attentively. In addition, effective listening will reduce the likelihood that we will misinterpret the message. Effective listening does not mean we are passively agreeing with the other person's message; instead, it means respecting the rights of the speaker to express his thoughts and feelings. Effective listening usually consists of:

- *paraphrasing* (or summarizing) the content of the message (e.g., "It sounds like you are really angry with me and want to avoid having a problem like this occur again")

- using *nonverbal communication* to show that you are attentive (e.g., making eye contact, leaning forward, saying "uh huh," etc.)

Stress that being open to others' comments and criticisms is much more effective in terms of fostering good communication than blowing up, refusing to listen, or accusing the other person of something in order to reduce one's own feelings of guilt or hurt.

Problem-Solving Conflicts

Finding Workable Solutions

Sometimes we must deal with situations that are more vague in terms of what the actual messages, desires, and feelings of the two parties are. Tell group members that they can apply what they have learned about making assertive statements to problem-solving conflicts using the following steps.

1. Recognize there is a problem and define it in clear terms. Be specific and avoid generalizations.

2. Identify possible solutions. Both parties should generate a variety of possible solutions.

3. Critique each possible solution. It is important to be assertive, but to remember that the best solution will meet both parties' needs.

4. Accept a solution. Both parties should discuss the expected outcomes and possible barriers to implementing the solution.

Non-Workable Solutions

There are often situations in which no workable solution is available or the risk of being assertive is too great. Tell the group that in these situations there are alternatives to directly assertive behavior, such as changing one's environment. They can use problem-focused strategies for changeable aspects and, especially, emotion-focused coping techniques to deal with unchangeable situations.

Assertiveness and Stress Management (5 minutes)

Explain that if a speaker's intentions are not clearly communicated then interpersonal conflict may occur. This conflict can be stressful. An important part of stress management, then, is learning how to communicate assertively. Assertiveness decreases stress by:

- allowing for a more efficient approach to dealing with situations

- allowing individuals to stand up for their rights without violating the rights of others

- allowing individuals to express personal likes and dislikes more easily

- allowing for clearer communication which leads to less emotional build-up

- making negotiation and disagreement less personal and unpleasant

- providing an opportunity for a person to disagree openly with another person

Facilitator Note

■ *Although assertive communication can be a useful stress management technique, it is important to understand that the choice of whether to use this form of communication in specific situations is up to the participant.* ■

It is not always best to be assertive. Assertiveness may be more or less appropriate in certain cultures and in certain situations. For example, asserting one's rights to someone who is angry, enraged, and not thinking clearly may only serve to escalate the person's anger. Explain that an important aspect of assertiveness is *timing* — knowing when an assertive message is most likely to result in positive and constructive change.

More on Assertiveness

You may also want to touch on the following points:

- People often confuse assertiveness with pushiness or aggressiveness.

- People who are thinking in "irrational" styles (e.g., overreacting, avoidance, black-and-white thinking) often have trouble being assertive.

- Assertive people are calm, direct, concerned about others, and usually gentle in their approach.

Common Barriers to Assertive Behavior (5 minutes)

Cognitive distortions can often keep us from behaving assertively. Remind the group that these examples represent inaccurate or negative thinking and can be disputed and replaced.

- "I may hurt someone."

- "I'll be rejected."

- "My job is to make people happy."

- "There must be a winner and a loser."

Review common patterns of distorted thinking that prevent assertive behavior as described here.

Fear of Rejection or Retaliation

Often our reaction to this fear is more immobilizing than the fear itself. When faced with the possibility of rejection or retaliation we often feel vulnerable and unsafe. This feeling can be manifested as anger and aggression. It is important to be aware of situations where we may feel vulnerable. In order to promote assertive behavior instead of aggressive behavior, it is important that we monitor our thoughts for negative self-statements and cognitive distortions, keeping in mind that we do not have to passively accept inappropriate treatment.

Mistaken Sense of Responsibility

When another person is hurt by our behavior, it is important to discern whether we actually hurt the other person or whether the other person felt hurt because of her own misinterpretation of our assertiveness. If we internalize others' hurt feelings and incorrectly interpret disapproval to mean that we are all bad, we are more likely to become depressed and less likely to stand up for our rights. It may also be important to assess what benefits we may gain when acting unassertively (e.g., by not standing up for our rights, people may defend us; by never disagreeing we can appear to be easy to get along with, etc.).

Mistaken View of Human Rights

Many people believe that they don't have the right to stand up for their wants, needs, and wishes. It is very difficult to be assertive when denying ourselves basic rights. It is important to remember that we can accept and act on our own rights without violating the rights of others.

Discussion Questions

- ■ "Did you identify with any of the common barriers to assertive behavior?"

- ■ "What are some of the reasons that you do not behave assertively?"

- ■ "When do you behave nonassertively?"

- ■ "Who are the people with whom you act nonassertively?"

- ■ "What are some advantages of acting nonassertively?"

- ■ "In what types of situations, or with what type of people, is it advisable to be nonassertive?"

Assertive Role-Play (5 minutes)

Have participants role-play assertive responses to the following scenarios.

Note: A copy of this exercise can be found in the participant workbook.

Scenario 1: *Ned has difficulty asking family and friends for assistance when he does not feel well. He doesn't want to be perceived as unable to accomplish tasks himself. He finds himself doing things that he is not well enough to do so that others will not know how ill he's feeling.*

- ■ *How might Ned assertively and confidently request assistance from others?*

- ■ *How might Ned respond when others deny his request for help?*

Scenario 2: *Mark just returned home from the hospital after surgery. He feels weak and tired. Many of his friends and relatives want to visit to see how he is doing. Mark just wants to rest with few distractions. He's feeling frustrated and angry because the house is full of people, and it is quite noisy.*

- ■ *How might Mark address this problem in an assertive manner?*

■ *How might Mark assertively express his negative feelings?*

Steps to More Assertive Behavior (5 minutes)

Review the following steps to assertive behavior with the group.

Step 1) Plan for change:
- Look at your rights, what you want, and what you need
- Examine the other person's rights, wants, and needs
- Arrange a time and place to discuss the situation

Step 2) Express yourself assertively:
- Define feelings using "I" messages
- Express your request simply, firmly, and concisely
- Reinforce the possibility of getting what you want by describing positive and negative consequences, but avoiding threats

Step 3) Listen effectively:
- Prepare: make sure you are ready to listen
- Listen and clarify
- Acknowledge: communicate to the other person that you have heard her position

Step 4) Find a solution:
- Understand that there may not be an immediate solution at that moment
- Give the other individual(s) time to process your dialogue
- Be prepared to process the other individual's comments, concerns, and arguments, and possibly revise your position

Homework (5 minutes)

✎ Have group members review session 9 of the workbook and complete the exercises.

✎ Have group members complete the Assertiveness Monitoring Sheet for two separate situations that occurred recently. If you'd like to provide group members with additional copies, you may photocopy this sheet from the workbook.

Session Evaluation (5 minutes) (optional)

Have group members complete the session evaluation sheet (see appendix).

Chapter 12

Session 10: Group Favorite Relaxation Exercise / Social Support and Program Wrap-Up

(Corresponds to session 10 of the workbook)

Materials Needed

- Flip chart or board

- Copy of participant workbook

- Comfortable chairs for relaxation training

- Copies of relaxation tapes (optional)

- Copies of monitoring sheets (optional)

- Copies of session and program evaluation sheets (optional)

RELAXATION TRAINING: *Group Favorite Relaxation Exercise*

Outline

- Discuss adherence to relaxation practice (5 minutes)

- Conduct group's favorite relaxation exercise (10–15 minutes depending on selected exercise)

- Discuss future relaxation practice (5 minutes)

Discussion of Adherence to Relaxation Practice (5 minutes)

Discuss obstacles or difficulties with relaxation practice. Ask the following questions:

■ "How often did you practice the relaxation exercise?"

■ "What barriers have you encountered?"

■ "Was there anything you could do to overcome these barriers?"

Optional: collect Relaxation Monitoring Sheets.

Group Favorite Relaxation Exercise (10–15 minutes)

Have the group select its favorite relaxation exercise to repeat for relaxation this session.

Discussion of Future Relaxation Practice (5 minutes)

Emphasize the importance of continuing the relaxation exercises, preferably on a daily basis. Also, explain that because participants will not be coming in on a weekly basis to report their relaxation exercise adherence, it is more likely that they may stop conducting the exercises. Ask the following:

■ "Have you made plans to continue conducting the relaxation exercises upon completion of the group?"

■ "Do you fully understand the mental and physical benefits of engaging in these exercises?"

■ "Can you draw support from a family member or friend, and perhaps team up, so you can continue doing these exercises?"

■ "Has anyone thought of putting together a calendar with days and times, and types of exercises they will engage in?"

Outline

- Check in with group members (5 minutes)

- Review material and homework from previous session (5 minutes)

- Introduce social support as a resource (5 minutes)

- Have group members complete social support exercise (5 minutes)

- Discuss the importance of matching types of social support with needs (5 minutes)

- Discuss variables and issues that may affect the quality of social support (10 minutes)

- Discuss social support for single men (10 minutes) (optional)

- Review possible strategies for enhancing quality of support network (5 minutes)

- Give wrap-up of program (10 minutes)

- Discuss group members' implementation of personal stress management programs (10 minutes)

- Conclude program and say goodbyes (5 minutes)

- Have group members complete session and program evaluation sheets (5–10 minutes)

Pre-Didactic Check-In (5 minutes)

Go around the room and have each group member share how he is doing and update other group members on any personal news.

Previous Material and Homework Review (5 minutes)

Review the material on assertive communication from the last session.

Review assigned stress management homework (e.g., Assertiveness Monitoring Sheet). Problem-solve any difficulties group members had completing the homework.

Introduction to Social Support (5 minutes)

Definition of Social Support

Social support consists of the psychological/emotional, informational, and tangible benefits we receive from our personal relationships. A social support network typically includes: family members (spouse/partner, children, grandchildren, parents, siblings), close friends, acquaintances (from clubs, religious organizations, and other activities), co-workers, and pets. You may want to ask group members to take a moment to think of the people who belong to their social support networks and the kinds of support they provide them.

Benefits of Social Support

Social support provides benefits in a number of domains.

In *non-stressful situations*, social support provides us with:

■ emotional/psychological benefits (warmth, intimacy, sharing accomplishments, self-esteem, self-identity, etc.)

In *stressful situations*, we may receive:

■ emotional/psychological benefits (consolation, comfort, alleviation from loneliness, etc.)

■ concrete/tangible help (information or access to information, help with chores, financial assistance, etc.)

Importance of Social Support to Stress Management

Explain that social support may intervene in the EVENT + APPRAISAL = EMOTION equation by attenuating or buffering the APPRAISAL. By reducing the emotional reaction, social support may help dampen physiological processes or maladaptive behaviors. Part of the appraisal process that we go through when we are faced with a stressful situation involves evaluating the types of resources we have to cope with the stressors. Available resources include other persons in our social network that would be helpful in facing the stressor. These individuals could be family, friends, or other persons with whom we have a supportive relationship and who are usually available in good and bad times.

Focus on the *quality* rather than *quantity* of social support. Quality social support is important because it:

- serves as a stress buffer and coping resource

- increases feelings of well-being

- provides a sense of predictability and stability in one's life

Types of Social Support

Prompt discussion of specific examples from the group and list on flip chart or board under the following headings. Add examples from the lists provided if not mentioned by the group.

Table 12.1. Examples of Types of Support

Psychological/Emotional	Informational	Tangible
encouragement, fun, consolation, affiliation, love, spirituality, prayer, sharing of concerns and fears, reduction of feelings of helplessness, being there for you so you do not feel overwhelmed	sharing of personal knowledge, assistance in research of needed material for decision-making, promotion of healthier behavior (often combined with professional support from doctors, nurses, etc.)	medical caretaking activities, help with household chores and other daily activities, financial support, work schedule accommodation, job sharing

Social Support Exercise (5 minutes)

Have group members complete the Social Support Exercise in the participant workbook. After they have completed the exercise, facilitate a group discussion about what they found out about their support networks that they were not aware of before doing this exercise. Ask about those people in their social network who have provided emotional, tangible, and/or informational support. Ask where they noted strengths and where they perceived weaknesses across these domains.

Matching Types of Social Support with Needs (5 minutes)

As with coping, if there is a match between one's needs and the types of social support provided, one will gain maximum benefits. Discuss matches and mismatches. You may want to use the following dialogue:

> *For example, you may have a friend that is a great source of support in regard to giving you a ride if your car is in the shop and to providing information on how to manage financial concerns. So this person can be viewed as a good source of tangible and informational support. However, this same individual may also not be very helpful on a day that you are feeling down. He may not know how to provide emotional support, hear you out, and so forth. This deficit does not diminish the importance of your friend but it is helpful to know that he is a good source of support for some issues, and not for others.*

Matching Exercise

Present the following situations to the group and have members evaluate the match between the need and the type of support provided.

Situation 1: *A friend or family member calls daily to find out if you "need to talk." You are feeling overwhelmed by medical decisions and treatments, work demands, and household chores.*

■ *What kind of support is the friend or family member offering?*

■ *What kind of support do you need?*

Situation 2: *You have made a decision about what medical treatment to undergo. Family members keep sending loads of information on choices open to you, alternative treatments, and new therapies.*

- *What kind of support are they offering?*

- *What kind of support do you need?*

Quality of Social Support (10 minutes)

General Variables

Several general variables influence the value/quality of the social support we receive. Review the following variables with group members and have them think about which ones may affect them. Just like matching the situation with the right source of support, it is important to be aware of other factors that have an impact on the quality of support available.

Accessibility: Geography, time or financial constraints

Attitude of supporters: A perceived lack of enthusiasm or initiation in the support offered by family and friends

Prior relationship patterns:
- strains and stresses within support group or individual relationships
- level of involvement or intimacy in personal relationships
- problems with matching need to help offered or available

Ability to ask for/receive help from others:
- presence of father/caretaker (breadwinner) syndrome
- tendency to withdraw when stressed
- concern with burdening or frightening others with one's fears
- fear of being perceived as unmanly/not masculine

Discuss common pitfalls with the group and use previous work on cognitive distortions to evaluate some of these thoughts and behaviors related to the ability to ask for/receive help from others.

Issues Specific to Individuals Living with Cancer

People are often frightened when they learn they have cancer. They fear the changes associated with the cancer, or its treatment. Sometimes, people may feel hostile toward others around them as they try to reconcile the meaning of the cancer in their lives. Tell group members that while this is a natural reaction, it can put a strain on relationships. Remind them that the diagnosis, treatment, and their aftereffects are also overwhelming and difficult for those who care for them.

Communicating feelings, fears, and needs is one way to prevent relationship difficulties. There are a number of ways for dealing with friends and relatives on the subject of one's cancer. You may want to introduce these with the following dialogue:

> *It can be difficult for some people to talk to you when they are aware that you have a serious illness like cancer. Many people do not know what to say and may feel fear and even avoid you. Some people may also overreact and become over involved. There are really no rights or wrongs when talking to others about your cancer. Keep in mind that everyone is different; each person has different experiences, different ways of coping with difficult situations, different personalities and interpersonal styles—all of which may affect how a person responds to you.*

The participant workbook contains several commonly accepted tips on how to approach others when talking about cancer. You may want to refer participants to their workbooks and review these as a group.

Particular Variables Which Might Affect Spouse/Partner Relationships

1. Communication difficulties:
    - fear of sharing a mutual fear of loss or making the "other one" feel worse
    - tendency to avoid each other or act "cheery" as defenses against these fears
    - lack of verbal or physical demonstrativeness (at a time when it may be especially desired)

2. Frustration and exhaustion with new strains on daily life due to illness

3. Fears of recurrence

4. Changes in physical intimacy patterns:
   - disruption due to treatment
   - possible changes in man's sensations
   - feelings about possible altered appearance or sexual functioning

Social Support and Single Men (optional) (10 minutes)

Facilitator Note

- *Check with group to see if any men are currently single. If not, skip this section.* ■

Social support networks are often different for men who are married/in partnerships versus those who are single. Single men may not have a close friend or family member they can rely on for emotional or tangible support as they would rely on a spouse. Some single men are also concerned about being rejected by a current or future lover because they've had cancer. In dating relationships, they may wish to appear brave and unaffected by the cancer. Sometimes they may even try to ignore that the cancer ever occurred. Emphasize, however, that good communication with dating partners is just as important as communication between spouses. This is especially important for relationships that may grow into marriage or life-partnership.

Role-Play for Single Men (optional)

If there are single men in the group, you may want to conduct the following role-play.

Situation: *Allen had a prostatectomy two years ago. He has been dating a woman, Sue, for one month, and she does not know that he had cancer. Things are starting to heat up sexually between them and Allen has decided to tell her about his cancer. How might Allen tell her that he had cancer in the past?*

Have a group member play the part of Allen and another the part of Allen's partner, Sue. Have participants use the following script:

Allen: *I'd like to tell you about something from my past that I have not mentioned before. I had prostate cancer a couple of years ago. I have had regular checkups from the doctor, and everything is okay, and I'm not concerned about a recurrence. How do you think that might affect our relationship?*

Sue: *Why did you never mention this before?*

Allen: *I guess that I hesitated to bring it up because I'm afraid you'd rather be with someone who hasn't had the disease. It also scares me to remember that time of my life. But I really want to know if you have any worries about my having had cancer.*

Sue: *What does this mean for our sex life? Are you able to get an erection? If you can't get an erection, there are still other sexual activities we can do together.*

The sad truth is that rejection is always a possibility. Remind single participants, however, that everyone gets rejected sometimes. Even without cancer, a person may reject another person for his looks, beliefs, personality, etc. Stress that the tragedy is when single people limit themselves by not dating out of fear. Negative self-talk decreases the possibility that they will enter into satisfying relationships and receive the social support they need.

Possible Strategies for Enhancing Quality of Support Network (5 minutes)

Encourage participants to strengthen their support networks with the following strategies.

Cognitive reassessment and restructuring. Ask yourself:

■ Am I willing to receive help?

■ Am I willing to ask for help?

- Are others willing to help me?

- Am I afraid to ask others?

- Do I need to be strong and manage on my own?

Answering "no" to the first three questions or "yes" to the last two questions indicates that cognitive restructuring techniques are needed to challenge thoughts that keep you from asking and receiving help.

Break down social support into individual components and take action on each. Match your needs with the type of support you elicit.

- Actively seek information as needed.

- Request or arrange for tangible help (e.g., chores, finances).

- Request time with family and friends for both illness-related and pleasure-related activities.

- Attempt more direct communication of feelings and needs with members of present network.

- Find new avenues of sharing and support (e.g. support groups, therapy or counseling, journaling, pets).

Program Wrap-Up (10 minutes)

Use the remainder of the session to finish up any material that was not covered, answer any questions, wrap up any loose ends, briefly review the content of the past ten weeks, and ask for feedback on the group experience.

The following chart (Table 12.2) can be used to review the goals of the program and the tools used to achieve them.

These goals and activities are all interdependent, creating a complete stress management package that allows one to draw upon several strategies at once for managing a given stressor. Use the following dialogue to illustrate this point:

> *For example, individuals experiencing poor social support might simultaneously seek to build their awareness of how being socially*

Table 12.2 Program Goals and Tools

GOAL	TOOLS
Awareness	Stress Monitoring, Body Scan
Appraisals	Cognitive Restructuring
Coping	Problem-focused and Emotion-focused Coping; Assertiveness, Anger Management, Relaxation
Resources	Social Network

> *isolated brings about various stress symptoms, examine how their distorted or negative thoughts prevent them from seeking out other people, determine how their passive coping strategies block them from solving interpersonal difficulties that keep them isolated, and finally, examine how their social support network might be expanded and changed to bring about more fulfilling interpersonal connections.*

Emphasize that for many stressors, employing several interconnected stress management techniques provides the most efficient strategy for dealing productively with problems and finding healthier solutions.

Use the following model of Cognitive-Behavioral Stress Management (CBSM) to demonstrate how these techniques can be used by individuals living with prostate cancer. (See Figure 12.1.)

Implementing Personal Stress Management Plans (10 minutes)

Emphasize that to maintain "Stress Management Fitness," group members must continue using the techniques learned in this program (just as they would have to continue exercising to maintain physical fitness). Use the following points and questions to lead a discussion about implementation and maintenance of a personal stress management program.

- "How do you plan to integrate stress management into your life?"

- "Do you see yourself as able to call upon the stress management tools you've learned?"

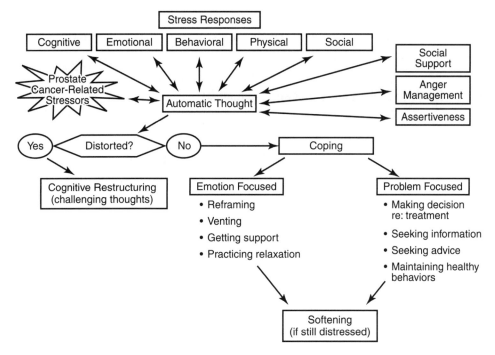

Figure 12.1.

CBSM Model of Stress Management for Prostate Cancer

■ "Are you able to envision a regular program of relaxation?"

■ "How will you begin this week? What tools will you use?"

These questions are also listed in the participant workbook under the section entitled "Your Personal Stress Management Plan."

Conclusion of Group (5 minutes)

Congratulate group members on completing the program. Reinforce their accomplishments and thank them for their participation. For additional support, refer them to the list of resources found in the participant workbook.

Encourage participants to say their good-byes to each other and exchange contact information if they would like to keep in touch.

Session / Program Evaluation (optional) (10 minutes)

Have group members complete the session evaluation sheet, as well as the overall program evaluation sheet (see appendix).

Session Evaluation Sheets

Session 1 Evaluation

Directions: For the first two items, write a number from 1 to 7, using the scale below.

1   2   3   4   5   6   7
Not at all   Very much

_____ 1. Your level of satisfaction with this group session.

_____ 2. Your desire to return to the next group session.

Directions: For the next item, circle how you feel on the the scale below.

RIGHT NOW, I FEEL . . .   1   2   3   4   5   6   7   8   9   10

	Very Relaxed	Neither Relaxed nor Stressed	Very Stressed

Directions: Answer the following questions by circling how you feel on the scale.

	Not At All				Extremely
1. How _anxious_ do you feel right now?	0	1	2	3	4
2. How _sad_ or _depressed_ do you feel right now?	0	1	2	3	4
3. How _confused_ do you feel right now?	0	1	2	3	4
4. How _energetic_ do you feel right now?	0	1	2	3	4
5. How _fatigued_ do you feel right now?	0	1	2	3	4
6. How _angry_ do you feel right now?	0	1	2	3	4

Directions: For the following items, write a number from 1 to 10, using the scale below.

Cannot do at all	Slightly certain	Moderately certain	Fairly certain	Completely certain
1 2	3 4	5 6	7 8	9 10

At this point in time, how confident or certain are you that you can . . .

_____ 1. Define what "stress" is?

_____ 2. Identify the symptoms of stress (physical, emotional, social, cognitive, behavioral)?

_____ 3. Identify situations where you feel stressed or upset?

_____ 4. Express how or what you really feel in group?

_____ 5. Practice your relaxation exercises at least once a day?

Session 2 Evaluation

Directions: For the first two items, write a number from 1 to 7, using the scale below.

1	2	3	4	5	6	7
Not at all						Very much

_____ 1. Your level of satisfaction with this group session.

_____ 2. Your desire to return to the next group session.

Directions: For the next item, circle how you feel on the the scale below.

RIGHT NOW, I FEEL . . .

1	2	3	4	5	6	7	8	9	10
Very Relaxed				Neither Relaxed nor Stressed					Very Stressed

Directions: Answer the following questions by circling how you feel on the scale.

	Not At All				Extremely
1. How *anxious* do you feel right now?	0	1	2	3	4
2. How *sad* or *depressed* do you feel right now?	0	1	2	3	4
3. How *confused* do you feel right now?	0	1	2	3	4
4. How *energetic* do you feel right now?	0	1	2	3	4
5. How *fatigued* do you feel right now?	0	1	2	3	4
6. How *angry* do you feel right now?	0	1	2	3	4

Directions: For the following items, write a number from 1 to 10, using the scale below.

Cannot do at all	Slightly certain	Moderately certain	Fairly certain	Completely certain
1　2	3　4	5　6	7　8	9　10

At this point in time, how confident or certain are you that you can . . .

_____ 1. Identify the physical effects of stress on your body?

_____ 2. Increase your awareness of the emotional effects of stress?

_____ 3. Increase your awareness of thoughts about events?

_____ 4. Express how or what you really feel in group?

_____ 5. Practice your relaxation exercises at least once a day?

Session 3 Evaluation

Directions: For the first two items, write a number from 1 to 7, using the scale below.

1   2   3   4   5   6   7
Not at all   Very much

_____ 1. Your level of satisfaction with this group session.

_____ 2. Your desire to return to the next group session.

Directions: For the next item, circle how you feel on the the scale below.

RIGHT NOW, I FEEL . . .   1   2   3   4   5   6   7   8   9   10
           Very   Neither Relaxed   Very
          Relaxed   nor Stressed   Stressed

Directions: Answer the following questions by circling how you feel on the scale.

	Not At All				Extremely
1. How *anxious* do you feel right now?	0	1	2	3	4
2. How *sad* or *depressed* do you feel right now?	0	1	2	3	4
3. How *confused* do you feel right now?	0	1	2	3	4
4. How *energetic* do you feel right now?	0	1	2	3	4
5. How *fatigued* do you feel right now?	0	1	2	3	4
6. How *angry* do you feel right now?	0	1	2	3	4

Directions: For the following items, write a number from 1 to 10, using the scale below.

Cannot do at all	Slightly certain	Moderately certain	Fairly certain	Completely certain
1 2	3 4	5 6	7 8	9 10

At this point in time, how confident or certain are you that you can . . .

_____ 1. Explain how your thoughts influence how you feel?

_____ 2. Identify your self-talk/automatic thoughts?

_____ 3. Be aware of your emotional state (identify how you feel)?

_____ 4. Express how or what you really feel in group?

_____ 5. Practice your relaxation exercises at least once a day?

Session 4 Evaluation

Directions: For the first two items, write a number from 1 to 7, using the scale below.

1	2	3	4	5	6	7
Not at all						Very much

_____ 1. Your level of satisfaction with this group session.

_____ 2. Your desire to return to the next group session.

Directions: For the next item, circle how you feel on the the scale below.

RIGHT NOW, I FEEL . . .

1	2	3	4	5	6	7	8	9	10
Very Relaxed				Neither Relaxed nor Stressed					Very Stressed

Directions: Answer the following questions by circling how you feel on the scale.

	Not At All				Extremely
1. How *anxious* do you feel right now?	0	1	2	3	4
2. How *sad* or *depressed* do you feel right now?	0	1	2	3	4
3. How *confused* do you feel right now?	0	1	2	3	4
4. How *energetic* do you feel right now?	0	1	2	3	4
5. How *fatigued* do you feel right now?	0	1	2	3	4
6. How *angry* do you feel right now?	0	1	2	3	4

Directions: For the following items, write a number from 1 to 10, using the scale below.

Cannot do at all	Slightly certain	Moderately certain	Fairly certain	Completely certain
1 2	3 4	5 6	7 8	9 10

At this point in time, how confident or certain are you that you can . . .

_____ 1. Recognize distorted thoughts?

_____ 2. Explain the connection between distorted thoughts and your emotional state?

_____ 3. Begin to change your negative thoughts?

_____ 4. Express how or what you really feel in group?

_____ 5. Practice your relaxation exercises at least once a day?

Session 5 Evaluation

Directions: For the first two items, write a number from 1 to 7, using the scale below.

1	2	3	4	5	6	7
Not at all						Very much

_____ 1. Your level of satisfaction with this group session.

_____ 2. Your desire to return to the next group session.

Directions: For the next item, circle how you feel on the the scale below.

RIGHT NOW, I FEEL . . .   1   2   3   4   5   6   7   8   9   10

Very Relaxed (1)   Neither Relaxed nor Stressed (5)   Very Stressed (10)

Directions: Answer the following questions by circling how you feel on the scale.

	Not At All				Extremely
1. How *anxious* do you feel right now?	0	1	2	3	4
2. How *sad* or *depressed* do you feel right now?	0	1	2	3	4
3. How *confused* do you feel right now?	0	1	2	3	4
4. How *energetic* do you feel right now?	0	1	2	3	4
5. How *fatigued* do you feel right now?	0	1	2	3	4
6. How *angry* do you feel right now?	0	1	2	3	4

Directions: For the following items, write a number from 1 to 10, using the scale below.

Cannot do at all		Slightly certain		Moderately certain		Fairly certain		Completely certain	
1	2	3	4	5	6	7	8	9	10

At this point in time, how confident or certain are you that you can . . .

_____ 1. Accurately evaluate your thoughts?

_____ 2. Explain the difference between balanced (rational) and unbalanced (irrational or rationalized) thoughts?

_____ 3. Effectively challenge and replace distorted negative thoughts?

_____ 4. Express how or what you really feel in group?

_____ 5. Practice your relaxation exercises at least once a day?

Session 6 Evaluation

Directions: For the first two items, write a number from 1 to 7, using the scale below.

$$1 \quad 2 \quad 3 \quad 4 \quad 5 \quad 6 \quad 7$$

Not at all   Very much

_____ 1. Your level of satisfaction with this group session.

_____ 2. Your desire to return to the next group session.

Directions: For the next item, circle how you feel on the the scale below.

RIGHT NOW, I FEEL . . .   1   2   3   4   5   6   7   8   9   10

Very Relaxed   Neither Relaxed nor Stressed   Very Stressed

Directions: Answer the following questions by circling how you feel on the scale.

	Not At All				Extremely
1. How *anxious* do you feel right now?	0	1	2	3	4
2. How *sad* or *depressed* do you feel right now?	0	1	2	3	4
3. How *confused* do you feel right now?	0	1	2	3	4
4. How *energetic* do you feel right now?	0	1	2	3	4
5. How *fatigued* do you feel right now?	0	1	2	3	4
6. How *angry* do you feel right now?	0	1	2	3	4

Directions: For the following items, write a number from 1 to 10, using the scale below.

Cannot do at all	Slightly certain	Moderately certain	Fairly certain	Completely certain
1 2	3 4	5 6	7 8	9 10

At this point in time, how confident or certain are you that you can . . .

_____ 1. Identify the controllable and uncontrollable parts of a major stressor?

_____ 2. Explain the difference between problem- and emotion-focused coping?

_____ 3. Identify and distinguish between active and passive coping styles?

_____ 4. Express how or what you really feel in group?

_____ 5. Practice your relaxation exercises at least once a day?

Session 7 Evaluation

Directions: For the first two items, write a number from 1 to 7, using the scale below.

$$1 \quad 2 \quad 3 \quad 4 \quad 5 \quad 6 \quad 7$$
Not at all   Very much

_____ 1. Your level of satisfaction with this group session.

_____ 2. Your desire to return to the next group session.

Directions: For the next item, circle how you feel on the the scale below.

RIGHT NOW, I FEEL . . .   1   2   3   4   5   6   7   8   9   10

Very   Neither Relaxed   Very
Relaxed   nor Stressed   Stressed

Directions: Answer the following questions by circling how you feel on the scale.

	Not At All				Extremely
1. How *anxious* do you feel right now?	0	1	2	3	4
2. How *sad* or *depressed* do you feel right now?	0	1	2	3	4
3. How *confused* do you feel right now?	0	1	2	3	4
4. How *energetic* do you feel right now?	0	1	2	3	4
5. How *fatigued* do you feel right now?	0	1	2	3	4
6. How *angry* do you feel right now?	0	1	2	3	4

Directions: For the following items, write a number from 1 to 10, using the scale below.

Cannot do at all	Slightly certain	Moderately certain	Fairly certain	Completely certain
1 2	3 4	5 6	7 8	9 10

At this point in time, how confident or certain are you that you can . . .

_____ 1. Identify the controllable and uncontrollable parts of a major stressor?

_____ 2. Explain the difference between problem- and emotion-focused coping?

_____ 3. Identify and distinguish between active and passive coping styles?

_____ 4. Express how or what you really feel in group?

_____ 5. Practice your relaxation exercises at least once a day?

Session 8 Evaluation

Directions: For the first two items, write a number from 1 to 7, using the scale below.

1   2   3   4   5   6   7
Not at all   Very much

_____ 1. Your level of satisfaction with this group session.

_____ 2. Your desire to return to the next group session.

Directions: For the next item, circle how you feel on the the scale below.

RIGHT NOW, I FEEL . . .   1   2   3   4   5   6   7   8   9   10
                   Very   Neither Relaxed   Very
             Relaxed   nor Stressed   Stressed

Directions: Answer the following questions by circling how you feel on the scale.

	Not At All				Extremely
1. How *anxious* do you feel right now?	0	1	2	3	4
2. How *sad* or *depressed* do you feel right now?	0	1	2	3	4
3. How *confused* do you feel right now?	0	1	2	3	4
4. How *energetic* do you feel right now?	0	1	2	3	4
5. How *fatigued* do you feel right now?	0	1	2	3	4
6. How *angry* do you feel right now?	0	1	2	3	4

Directions: For the following items, write a number from 1 to 10, using the scale below.

Cannot do at all	Slightly certain	Moderately certain	Fairly certain	Completely certain
1 2	3 4	5 6	7 8	9 10

At this point in time, how confident or certain are you that you can . . .

_____ 1. Monitor your thoughts associated with anger?

_____ 2. Decrease your angry feelings?

_____ 3. Increase your awareness of the physical effects of anger?

_____ 4. Express how or what you really feel in group?

_____ 5. Practice your relaxation exercises at least once a day?

Session 9 Evaluation

Directions: For the first two items, write a number from 1 to 7, using the scale below.

1   2   3   4   5   6   7
Not at all   Very much

_____ 1. Your level of satisfaction with this group session.

_____ 2. Your desire to return to the next group session.

Directions: For the next item, circle how you feel on the the scale below.

RIGHT NOW, I FEEL . . .   1   2   3   4   5   6   7   8   9   10
                     Very   Neither Relaxed   Very
                  Relaxed   nor Stressed   Stressed

Directions: Answer the following questions by circling how you feel on the scale.

	Not At All				Extremely
1. How *anxious* do you feel right now?	0	1	2	3	4
2. How *sad* or *depressed* do you feel right now?	0	1	2	3	4
3. How *confused* do you feel right now?	0	1	2	3	4
4. How *energetic* do you feel right now?	0	1	2	3	4
5. How *fatigued* do you feel right now?	0	1	2	3	4
6. How *angry* do you feel right now?	0	1	2	3	4

Directions: For the following items, write a number from 1 to 10, using the scale below.

Cannot   Slightly   Moderately   Fairly   Completely
do at all   certain   certain   certain   certain
1   2   3   4   5   6   7   8   9   10

At this point in time, how confident or certain are you that you can . . .

_____ 1. Differentiate between the four types of interpersonal communication styles (aggressive, passive, passive-aggressive, assertive)?

_____ 2. Be appropriately assertive when you need to be?

_____ 3. Tell others how you feel without hurting or offending them?

_____ 4. Express how or what you really feel in group?

_____ 5. Practice your relaxation exercises at least once a day?

Session 10 Evaluation

Directions: For the first two items, write a number from 1 to 7, using the scale below.

1	2	3	4	5	6	7
Not at all					Very much	

_____ 1. Your level of satisfaction with this group session.

_____ 2. Your desire to return to the next group session.

Directions: For the next item, circle how you feel on the the scale below.

RIGHT NOW, I FEEL . . .   1   2   3   4   5   6   7   8   9   10

Very Relaxed	Neither Relaxed nor Stressed	Very Stressed

Directions: Answer the following questions by circling how you feel on the scale.

		Not At All				Extremely
1.	How *anxious* do you feel right now?	0	1	2	3	4
2.	How *sad* or *depressed* do you feel right now?	0	1	2	3	4
3.	How *confused* do you feel right now?	0	1	2	3	4
4.	How *energetic* do you feel right now?	0	1	2	3	4
5.	How *fatigued* do you feel right now?	0	1	2	3	4
6.	How *angry* do you feel right now?	0	1	2	3	4

Directions: For the following items, write a number from 1 to 10, using the scale below.

Cannot do at all	Slightly certain	Moderately certain	Fairly certain	Completely certain
1 2	3 4	5 6	7 8	9 10

At this point in time, how confident or certain are you that you can . . .

_____ 1. Explain the benefits of social support?

_____ 2. Identify the people in your life who provide you with social support (e.g. emotional, informational, tangible)?

_____ 3. Get support from others when you need it?

_____ 4. Monitor and evaluate your thinking?

_____ 5. Manage your emotions?

_____ 6. Practice your coping skills?

Overall Program Evaluation

Directions: For the followings items, please use the scale below to rate the degree to which you found the information helpful.

1   2   3   4   5   6   7

Not at all   Very much

_____ 1. Increasing your awareness of the negative effects of stress.

_____ 2. Learning to identify and replace distorted thoughts with more rational thoughts (cognitive restructuring).

_____ 3. Learning how to appropriately match your coping response to the specific situation.

_____ 4. Learning how to manage your anger.

_____ 5. Learning assertiveness skills.

_____ 6. Learning how to increase your social support.

OPTIONAL: Please give any other comments, suggestions, or criticisms that you feel would improve the quality of the group sessions.

Fidelity Checklists

Session 1 – Fidelity Checklist

Group: _____ Date: _____

Rate your fidelity to each session element on a scale of 1 to 7, with 1 indicating poor fidelity and 7 indicating high fidelity.

Introduction to the Program   Actual Time:

_____ Introduce co-leaders and provide positive reinforcement (5 minutes)   _____

_____ Present general program information (15 minutes)   _____

_____ Conduct reporter exercise (15 minutes)   _____

_____ Describe structure of the program (10 minutes)   _____

_____ Provide information about prostate cancer (25 minutes)   _____

Stress Management: *Stress Awareness and Physical Responses*   Actual Time:

_____ Define stress (5 minutes)   _____

_____ Describe the effects of stress (10 minutes)   _____

_____ Have group members complete the symptoms of stress checklist   _____
(5 minutes)

_____ Discuss the physical effects of stress (10 minutes)   _____

_____ Review the link between stress and cancer (5 minutes)   _____

_____ Discuss optional topics: _____(5 minutes)   _____

_____ Assign homework (5 minutes)   _____

Relaxation Training: *8-Muscle-Group Progressive Muscle Relaxation*   Actual Time:

_____ Introduce progressive muscle relaxation and give rationale (10 minutes)   _____

_____ Review procedure and muscle groups for progressive muscle relaxation   _____
(10 minutes)

_____ Conduct 8-Muscle-Group Progressive Muscle Relaxation (20 minutes)   _____

_____ Discuss relaxation experience and today's session (5 minutes)   _____

_____ Assign homework (5 minutes)   _____

_____ Have group members complete session evaluation sheet (5 minutes)   _____
(optional)

Notes:

Session 2 – Fidelity Checklist

Group: _____ Date: _____

Rate your fidelity to each session element on a scale of 1 to 7, with 1 indicating poor fidelity and 7 indicating high fidelity.

Relaxation Training: *Diaphragmatic Breathing and 4-Muscle-Group Progressive Muscle Relaxation*　　　Actual Time:

_____ Discuss adherence to relaxation practice (5 minutes)　　　_____

_____ Introduce diaphragmatic breathing and give rationale (5 minutes)　　　_____

_____ Conduct diaphragmatic breathing exercise (10 minutes)　　　_____

_____ Conduct progressive muscle relaxation for four muscle groups (15 minutes)　　　_____

_____ Discuss relaxation practice (3 minutes)　　　_____

_____ Assign homework (2 minutes)　　　_____

Stress Management: *Stress Awareness and the Appraisal Process*　　　Actual Time:

_____ Check in with group members (5 minutes)　　　_____

_____ Review material and homework from the previous session (5 minutes)　　　_____

_____ Discuss the importance of awareness to stress management (5 minutes)　　　_____

_____ Review the negative effects of stress (5 minutes)　　　_____

_____ Create awareness of physical tension and sensations (20 minutes)　　　_____

_____ Introduce the appraisal process (10 minutes)　　　_____

_____ Discuss the connection between appraisals, emotions, and reactions (10 minutes)　　　_____

_____ Practice the appraisal process (10 minutes)　　　_____

_____ Assign homework (5 minutes)　　　_____

_____ Have group members complete session evaluation sheet (5 minutes) (optional)　　　_____

Notes:

Session 3 – Fidelity Checklist

Group: _____ Date: _____

Rate your fidelity to each session element on a scale of 1 to 7, with 1 indicating poor fidelity and 7 indicating high fidelity.

Relaxation Training: *Deep Breathing and Counting with Passive Progressive Muscle Relaxation*   Actual Time:

_____ Discuss adherence to relaxation practice (5 minutes)   _____

_____ Introduce deep breathing and counting (5 minutes)   _____

_____ Introduce passive progressive muscle relaxation (5 minutes)   _____

_____ Conduct deep breathing and counting with passive
4-Muscle-Group PMR (15 minutes)   _____

_____ Discuss relaxation practice (3 minutes)   _____

_____ Assign homework (2 minutes)   _____

Stress Management: *Sex and Sexuality After Prostate Cancer Treatment and Automatic Thoughts*   Actual Time:

_____ Check in with group members (5 minutes)   _____

_____ Discuss sex and sexuality after prostate cancer treatment (10 minutes)   _____

_____ Encourage expansion of sexual repertoire (10 minutes)   _____

_____ Discuss HIV and how to protect oneself (5 minutes)   _____

_____ Review material and homework from previous session (5 minutes)   _____

_____ Discuss the functions of emotion/self-talk linkage (5 minutes)   _____

_____ Teach how to break the cycle of negative thoughts and feelings
(10 minutes)   _____

_____ Discuss linking exercise (5 minutes)   _____

_____ Assign homework (5 minutes)   _____

_____ Have group members complete session evaluation sheet (5 minutes)   _____
(optional)

Notes:

Session 4 – Fidelity Checklist

Group: _____   Date: _____

Rate your fidelity to each session element on a scale of 1 to 7, with 1 indicating poor fidelity and 7 indicating high fidelity.

Relaxation Training: *Special Place Imagery*   Actual Time:

_____ Discuss adherence to relaxation practice (5 minutes)   _____

_____ Introduce special place imagery (5 minutes)   _____

_____ Conduct passive PMR with special place imagery exercise (20 minutes)   _____

_____ Discuss relaxation practice (3 minutes)   _____

_____ Assign homework (2 minutes)   _____

Stress Management: *Cognitive Distortions*   Actual Time:

_____ Check in with group members (5 minutes)   _____

_____ Review material and homework from the previous session (5 minutes)   _____

_____ Introduce types of negative thinking/cognitive distortions (10 minutes)   _____

_____ Discuss how negative thoughts influence behavior (5 minutes) _____

_____ Have group members practice labeling negative thoughts (10 minutes)   _____

_____ Review possible areas of negative thoughts (5 minutes)   _____

_____ Conduct group discussion on negative thoughts (10 minutes)   _____

_____ Discuss changing negative thoughts about sexuality (5 minutes)   _____

_____ Assign homework (5 minutes)   _____

_____ Have group members complete session evaluation sheet (5 minutes) (optional)   _____

Notes:

Session 5 – Fidelity Checklist

Group: _____ Date: _____

Rate your fidelity to each session element on a scale of 1 to 7, with 1 indicating poor fidelity and 7 indicating high fidelity.

Relaxation Training: *Relaxation for Healing and Well-Being*   Actual Time:

_____ Discuss adherence to relaxation practice (5 minutes)   _____

_____ Introduce relaxation exercise for healing and well-being (5 minutes)   _____

_____ Conduct relaxation exercise (15 minutes)   _____

_____ Discuss relaxation exercise (3 minutes)   _____

_____ Assign homework (2 minutes)   _____

Stress Management: *Cognitive Restructuring*   Actual Time:

_____ Check in with group members (5 minutes)   _____

_____ Review material and homework from previous session (5 minutes)   _____

_____ Introduce irrational, rational, and rationalized thoughts (10 minutes)   _____

_____ Have group members practice identifying self-talk (10 minutes)   _____

_____ Conduct role-play of irrational, rational, and rationalized responses   _____
           (5 minutes)

_____ Teach how to replace negative thoughts with more rational responses   _____
           (10 minutes)

_____ Have group practice the steps to thought replacement (10 minutes)   _____

_____ Review helpful guidelines for generating rational responses (5 minutes)   _____

_____ Assign homework (5 minutes)   _____

_____ Have group members complete session evaluation sheet (5 minutes)   _____
           (optional)

Notes:

Session 6 – Fidelity Checklist

Group: _____ Date: _____

Rate your fidelity to each session element on a scale of 1 to 7, with 1 indicating poor fidelity and 7 indicating high fidelity.

Relaxation Training: *Autogenic Training*   Actual Time:

_____ Discuss adherence to relaxation practice (5 minutes)   _____

_____ Introduce autogenic training (10 minutes)   _____

_____ Conduct autogenic exercises for heaviness and warmth (10 minutes)   _____

_____ Discuss relaxation practice (3 minutes)   _____

_____ Assign homework (2 minutes)   _____

Stress Management: *Coping I*   Actual Time:

_____ Check in with group members (5 minutes)   _____

_____ Review material and homework from previous session (5 minutes)   _____

_____ Define coping (10 minutes)   _____

_____ Discuss controllable versus uncontrollable aspects of a situation   _____
(5 minutes)

_____ Discuss problem-focused versus emotion-focused coping (5 minutes)   _____

_____ Discuss the importance of a fit between the controllability of a stressor _____
and the coping strategy (5 minutes)

_____ Discuss active versus passive approaches to coping (5 minutes)   _____

_____ Conduct coping exercise (5 minutes)   _____

_____ Review the coping process (5 minutes)   _____

_____ Help group members identify their personal coping styles (10 minutes)   _____

_____ Review steps for matching coping responses to the situation (5 minutes) _____

_____ Review coping's place in the stress management model (5 minutes)   _____

_____ Assign homework (5 minutes)   _____

_____ Have group members complete session evaluation sheet (5 minutes)   _____
(optional)

Notes:

Session 7 – Fidelity Checklist

Group: _____ Date: _____

Rate your fidelity to each session element on a scale of 1 to 7, with 1 indicating poor fidelity and 7 indicating high fidelity.

Relaxation Training: *Autogenics with Visual Imagery and*
Positive Self-Suggestions   Actual Time:

_____ Discuss adherence to relaxation practice (5 minutes)   _____

_____ Introduce autogenics with visual imagery and positive self-suggestions   _____
(5 minutes)

_____ Conduct autogenic exercises (10 minutes)   _____

_____ Conduct visual imagery and positive self-suggestions exercise   _____
(10 minutes)

_____ Discuss relaxation practice (3 minutes)   _____

_____ Assign homework (2 minutes)   _____

Stress Management: *Coping II*   Actual Time:

_____ Check in with group members (5 minutes)   _____

_____ Review material and homework from previous session (15 minutes)   _____

_____ Recite Serenity Prayer (5 minutes)   _____

_____ Introduce the concept of acceptance/softening (5 minutes)   _____

_____ Conduct softening exercise (10 minutes)   _____

_____ Review coping's place in the stress management model (10 minutes)   _____

_____ Discuss coping exercise for controllable and uncontrollable aspects   _____
(10 minutes)

_____ Assign homework (5 minutes)   _____

_____ Have group members complete session evaluation sheet (5 minutes)   _____
(optional)

Notes:

Session 8 – Fidelity Checklist

Group: _____   Date: _____

Rate your fidelity to each session element on a scale of 1 to 7, with 1 indicating poor fidelity and 7 indicating high fidelity.

Relaxation Training: *Mantra Meditation*   Actual Time:

_____ Discuss adherence to relaxation practice (5 minutes)   _____

_____ Introduce meditation (10 minutes)   _____

_____ Review instructions for mantra meditation (15 minutes)   _____

_____ Conduct mantra meditation exercise (10 minutes)   _____

_____ Discuss meditation practice (5 minutes)   _____

_____ Assign homework (2 minutes)   _____

Stress Management: *Anger Management*   Actual Time:

_____ Check in with group members (5 minutes)   _____

_____ Review material and homework from previous session (5 minutes)   _____

_____ Discuss anger awareness (10 minutes)   _____

_____ Have group members complete the Self-Evaluation Questionnaire   _____
        (5 minutes)

_____ Discuss unhealthy ways to express anger (10 minutes)   _____

_____ Have group recognize anger behaviors (5 minutes)   _____

_____ Discuss the importance of awareness of dynamics and other factors   _____
        (5 minutes)

_____ Review the consequences of anger (5 minutes)   _____

_____ Teach how to change maladaptive anger patterns (10 minutes)   _____

_____ Assign homework (5 minutes)   _____

_____ Have group members complete session evaluation sheet (5 minutes)   _____
        (optional)

Notes:

Session 9 – Fidelity Checklist

Group: _____ Date: _____

Rate your fidelity to each session element on a scale of 1 to 7, with 1 indicating poor fidelity and 7 indicating high fidelity.

Relaxation Training: *Mindfulness Meditation*   Actual Time:

_____ Discuss adherence to relaxation practice (5 minutes)   _____

_____ Introduce mindfulness meditation (5 minutes)   _____

_____ Conduct mindfulness meditation exercise (20 minutes)   _____

_____ Discuss meditation practice (3 minutes)   _____

_____ Assign homework (2 minutes)   _____

Stress Management: *Assertive Communication*   Actual Time:

_____ Check in with group members (5 minutes)   _____

_____ Review material and homework from previous session (5 minutes)   _____

_____ Present the four basic interpersonal styles (10 minutes)   _____

_____ Have group members role-play interpersonal styles (5 minutes)   _____

_____ Introduce the components of assertive communication (10 minutes)   _____

_____ Discuss the importance of assertiveness to stress management
(5 minutes)   _____

_____ Discuss common barriers to assertive behavior (5 minutes)   _____

_____ Have group members role-play assertive responses (5 minutes)   _____

_____ Review steps to more assertive behavior (5 minutes)   _____

_____ Assign homework (5 minutes)   _____

_____ Have group members complete session evaluation sheet (5 minutes)
(optional)   _____

Notes:

Session 10 – Fidelity Checklist

Group: _____ Date: _____

Rate your fidelity to each session element on a scale of 1 to 7, with 1 indicating poor fidelity and 7 indicating high fidelity.

Relaxation Training: *Group Favorite Relaxation Exercise*   Actual Time:

_____ Discuss adherence to relaxation practice (5 minutes)   _____

_____ Conduct group's favorite relaxation exercise: _____   _____
(10–15 minutes depending on selected exercise)

_____ Discuss future relaxation practice (5 minutes)   _____

Stress Management: *Social Support and Program Wrap-Up*   Actual Time:

_____ Check in with group members (5 minutes)   _____

_____ Review material and homework from previous session (5 minutes)   _____

_____ Introduce social support as a resource (5 minutes)   _____

_____ Have group members complete social support exercise (5 minutes)   _____

_____ Discuss the importance of matching types of social support with   _____
needs (5 minutes)

_____ Discuss variables and issues that may affect the quality of social   _____
support (10 minutes)

_____ Discuss social support for single men (10 minutes) (optional)   _____

_____ Review possible strategies for enhancing quality of support network   _____
(5 minutes)

_____ Give wrap-up of program (10 minutes)   _____

_____ Discuss group members' implementation of personal stress   _____
management programs (10 minutes)

_____ Conclude program and say goodbyes (5 minutes)   _____

_____ Have group members complete session and program evaluation   _____
sheets (5–10 minutes)

Notes:

References

American Cancer Society. (n.d.). Overview prostate cancer survival rates. Retrieved July 17, 2007, from http://www.cancer.org

American Cancer Society. (2007). *Cancer facts & figures 2007.* Atlanta: American Cancer Society.

Amling, C. L., Riffenburgh, R. H., Sun, L., Moul, J. W., Lance, R. S., & Kusuda, L., et al. (2003). Pathologic variables and recurrence rates as related to obesity and race in men with prostate cancer undergoing radical prostatectomy. *Journal of Clinical Oncology, 22*(3), 439–445.

Andersen, B. L. (1992). Psychological interventions for cancer patients to enhance quality of life. *Journal of Consulting Clinical Psychology, 60*(4), 552–568.

Antoni, M. H. (2003). Stress management effects on psychological, endocrinological and immune function in men with HIV: Empirical support for a psychoneuroimmunological model. *Stress, 6,* 173–188.

Antoni M. H., Lehman J. M., Kilbourn K. M., Boyers, A.E., Culver J. L., & Alferi, S. M., et al. (2001). Cognitive-behavioral stress management intervention decreases the prevalence of depression and enhances benefit finding among women under treatment for early-stage breast cancer. *Health Psycholology, 20*(1), 20–32.

Antoni, M. H., Schneiderman, N., & Penedo, F. J. (2006). Behavioral interventions and psychoneuroimmunology. In R. Ader, R. Glaser, N. Cohen, & M. Irwin (Eds.), Psychoneuroimmunology (4th Ed). New York: Academic Press.

Balderson, N., & Towell, T. (2003). The prevalence and predictors of psychological distress in men with prostate cancer who are seeking support. *British Journal of Health Psychology, 8*(125), 134.

Benson, H. (1975). *The relaxation response.* New York: Avon Books.

Bernstein, B., & Borkovec, T. (1973). *Progressive relaxation training: A manual for the helping professions.* Champaign, IL: Research Press.

Burns, D. (1981). *Feeling good: The new mood therapy.* New York: New American Library.

Cohen, S., Doyle, W. J., Skoner, D. P. (1999). Psychological stress, cytokine production, and severity of upper respiratory illness. *Psychosomatic Medicine, 61,* 175–180.

Cruess, D. G., Antoni, M. H., McGregor, B.A., Kilbourn, K. M., Boyers, A. E., & Alferi, S. M., *et al.* (2000). Cognitive-behavioral stress management reduces serum cortisol by enhancing benefit finding among women being treated for early stage breast cancer. *Psychosomatic Medicine, 62*(3), 304–308.

Davis, M., Eshelman, E. R., McKay, M., & Winemiller, V. (1988). *The relaxation & stress reduction workbook* (3rd Ed.). Oakland, CA: New Harbinger Publications.

Eton, D. T., & Lepore, S. J. (2002). Prostate cancer and health-related quality of life: a review of the literature. *Psycho-Oncology, 11,* 307–326.

Eton, D. T., Lepore, S. J., & Helgeson, V. S. (2001). Early quality of life in patients with localized prostate carcinoma: An examination of treatment-related, demographic, and psychosocial factors. *Cancer, 15*(6), 1451–1459.

Fawzy, F., Fawzy, N., Hyun, C., Elashoff, R., Guthrie, D., Fahey, J., & Morton, D. (1993). Malignant melanoma. Effects of an early structured psychiatric intervention, coping and affective state on recurrence and survival 6 years later. *Archives of General Psychiatry, 50*(9), 681–689.

Fawzy, F. I., Fawzy, N. W., Hyun, C. S., & Wheeler, J. G. (1997). Brief coping-oriented therapy for patients with malignant melanoma. In J. L. Spira (Ed.), *Group therapy for medically ill patients.* New York: Guilford Press.

Florida Department of Health. (n.d.). Retrieved July 17, 2007, from http://www.doh.state.fl.us/Disease_ctrl/std/clinical/stdcontrol.html

Folkman, J., Szabo, S., Stovroff, M., McNeil, P., Li, W., & Shing, Y. (1991). Duodenal ulcer. Discovery of a new mechanism and development of angiogenic therapy that accelerates healing. *Annals of Surgery, 214*(4), 414–425.

Gregoire, I., Kalogeropoulos, D., & Corcos, J. (1997). The effectiveness of a professionally led support group for men with prostate cancer. *Urology Nursing, 17*(2), 58–66.

Hadley, J., & Staudacher, C. (1996). *Hypnosis for change* (3rd Ed.). Oakland, CA: New Harbinger Publications.

The Health Central Network. (2004). Retrieved July 17, 2007, from http://www.drkoop.com/encyclopedia/93/182.html

Ironson, G. Lutgendorf, S., Starr, K. & Costello, N. (1989). *Anger management skills training,* Unpublished manuscript. University of Miami, Coral Gables, FL.

Kabat-Zinn, J. (1990). *Full catastrophe living: Using the wisdom of your body and mind to face stress, pain, and illness.* New York: Dell Publishing.

Lazarus, R. S., & Folkman, S. (1984). *Stress, appraisal, and coping.* New York: Springer.

Lepore, S., & Helgeson, V. S. (1998). Social constraints, intrusive thoughts and mental health after prostate cancer. *Journal of Social and Clinical psychology, 17*(1), 89-106.

Lepore, S. J., Eton D. V, Helgeson, V. S., & Schulz, R. (2003). Improving quality of life in men with prostate cancer: A randomized controlled trial of group education interventions. *Health Psychology, 22*(5), 443–452.

Luecken, L. J. & Compas, B. E. (2002). Stress, coping, and immune function in breast cancer. *Annals of Behavioral Medicine, 24,* 336–344.

Mason, L. J. (1985). *Guide to stress reduction.* Berkeley, CA: Celestial Arts.

McCaul, K. D., Solomon, S., & Holmes, D. S. (1976). Effects of paced respiration and expectations on physiological and psychological responses to threat. *Journal of Personality and Social Psychology, 37*(4), 564–571.

Meyer, T. J. & Mark, M. M. (1995). Effects of psychosocial interventions with adult cancer patients: A meta-analysis of randomized experiments. *Health Pscholology, 14*(2), 101–108.

Miller, K. M. (1987). Deep breathing relaxation. A pain management technique. *Association of Operating Room Nurses Journal, 45*(2), 484–488.

Mishel, M. H., Belyea, M., Germino, B. B., Stewart, J. L., Bailey, D. E., Robertson C., & Mohler, J. (2002). Helping patients with localized prostate carcinoma manage uncertainty and treatment side effects. *Cancer, 94*(6), 1854–1866

Molton, I., Siegel, S. D., Penedo, F. J., Dahn, J. R., Kinsinger, D., Schneiderman, N., & Antoni, M. H. (2007). Promoting recovery of sexual functioning after radical prostatectomy with group-based stress management: The role of interpersonal sensitivity. *Journal of Psychosomatic Research,* In Press.

Penedo, F. J., Dahn, J. R, Gonzalez, J. S., Molton, I., Thomas, E., Lechner, S., Schneiderman, N., Gheiler, E., & Roos, B. (2002). Cognitive-behavioral stress management (CBSM) enhances coping and reduces psychological distress in men who underwent radical prostatectomy for Stages I-II prostate cancer. *Psychosomatic Medicine, 64*(1), 159.

Penedo, F. J., Dahn, J. R., Molton, I., Gonzalez, J., Roos, B., Schneiderman, N., & Antoni, M. (2004a). Cognitive-behavioral stress management improves quality of life and stress management skill in men treated for localized prostate cancer. *Cancer, 100*(1), 192–200.

Penedo, F. J. & Dahn, J. R. (2004b). Prostate cancer and quality of life: A review and evaluation of the impact of treatment, disease burden and psychosocial interventions. *Expert Review of Pharmacoeconomics and Outcomes Research, 4*(5), 525–535.

Penedo, F. J., Molton, I., Dahn, J. R., Shen, B. J., Kinsinger, D., Traeger, L., Siegel, S., Schneiderman, N., & Antoni, M. (2006). A randomized clinical trial of group-based cognitive-behavioral stress management (CBSM) in localized prostate cancer: Development of stress management skills improves quality of life and benefit finding. *Annals of Behavioral Medicine, 31*(3), 261–270

Penedo, F. J., Dahn, J. R., Shen, B. J., Schneiderman, N., & Antoni, M. H. (2006). Ethnicity and determinants of quality of life after prostate cancer treatment. *Urology, 67*(5), 1022–1027.

Penedo, F. J., Dahn, J. R., Gonzalez, J. S., Molton, I., Carver, C. S., Antoni, M. H., Roos, B. A., & Schneiderman, N. (2003). Perceived stress management skill mediates the relationship between optimism and positive mood following radical prostatectomy. *Health Psychology, 22*(2), 220–222.

Penson, D. F., Ziding, F., Kuniyuki, A., McClerran, D., Albertsen, C., Deapen, D., et al. (2003). General quality of life 2 years following treatment for prostate cancer: What influences outcomes? Results from the prostate cancer outcome study. *Journal of Clinical Oncology, 21*(6), 1147–1154.

Peyromaure, M., Ravery, V., Boccon-Gibod, L. (2002). The management of stress urinary incontinence after radical prostatectomy. *British Journal of Urology International, 90*, 155–161.

Potosky, A. L., Davis, W. W., Hoffman, R. M., Stanford, J. L., Stephenson, R. A., & Penson, D. F., et al. (2004). Five-year outcomes after prostatectomy or radiotherapy for prostate cancer: The Prostate Cancer Outcomes Study. *Journal of the National Cancer Institute, 96*(18), 1358–1367.

Ptacek, J. T., Pierce, G. R., Ptacek, J. J., & Nogel, C. (1999). Stress and coping processes in men with prostate cancer: The divergent views of husbands and wives. *Journal of Social and Clinical Psychology, 18*, 299–324.

Schover, L. R., Fouladi, R. T., Warneke, C. L., Neese, L., Klein, E. A., Zippe, C., et al. (2002). Defining sexual outcomes after treatment for localized prostate carcinoma. *Cancer, 95*(8), 1773–1785.

Segerstrom, S. & Miller, G. (2004). Psychological stress and the human immune system: A meta-analytic study of 30 years of inquiry. *Psychological Bulletin, 130*, 601–630.

Simonton, J. T. (1978). Practical ptosis surgery. The Wendell L. Hughes Lecture. *Ophthalmology, 85*(8), 763–765.

Spiegel, D., Yalom, I. D. (1978). A support group for dying patients. *International Journal of Group Psychotherapy, 28*(2), 233–245.

Stanford, J. L., Feng, Z., Hamilton, A. S., Gilliland, F. D., Stephenson, R. A., Eley, J. W., et al. (2000). Urinary and sexual function after radical prostatectomy for clinically localized prostate cancer: the prostate cancer outcomes study. *JAMA, 283*(3), 354-360.

Traeger, L., Penedo, F. J., Gonzalez, J. S., Dahn, J., Lechner, S., Schneiderman, N., & Antoni, M. H. (2008). Illness perceptions and quality of life in men treated for localized prostate cancer. *Journal of Psychosomatic Research,* Under Review.

Wei, J. T., Dunn, R. L., Sandler, H. M., McLaughlin, P. W., Montie, J. E., Litwin, M. S., et al. (2002). Comprehensive comparison of health-related quality of life after contemporary therapies for localized prostate cancer. *Journal of Clinical Oncology, 20,* 557–566.

Zabora, J., Brintzenhofeszoc, K., Curbow, B., Hooker, C., & Piantadosi, S. (2001). The prevalence of psychological distress by cancer site. *Psycho-Oncology, 10*(1), 19–28.

About the Authors

Frank J. Penedo, Ph.D., is a clinical health psychologist and associate professor at the University of Miami, Department of Psychology, and the University of Miami Sylvester Comprehensive Cancer Center (SCCC), Division of Biobehavioral Oncology and Cancer Epidemiology. He is also a member of Geriatrics Research Education and Clinical Center (GRECC) at the Miami VAMC and the University of Miami Center on Aging.

Dr. Penedo has served as a project leader or principal investigator in several NCI-funded studies addressing biobehavioral correlates of adjustment, quality of life interventions, and health disparities across various cancer populations, with a primary focus on prostate cancer. He has also conducted cultural and linguistic translations of quality of life interventions for cancer survivors. Currently he leads an NCI-funded study evaluating the efficacy of psychosocial group interventions in improving quality of life and disease status in advanced prostate cancer. He is also the P.I. of a study addressing psychosocial, ethnic, and biobehavioral determinants of quality of life and adjustment in prostate cancer. Dr. Penedo also serves as Co-P.I. of an NCI study designed to assess biobehavioral factors related to progression in ovarian cancer, and he is the Southeast U.S. Co-P.I. of an NCI-funded Community Network Program (*Redes en Accion:* The Latino Cancer Research Network) specifically designed to raise primary and secondary cancer prevention awareness, research and training among Hispanic/Latinos. As part of the Behavioral Medicine Research Center in the University of Miami Department of Psychology, he has led several NIMH-funded studies evaluating the efficacy of group-based psychosocial interventions in improving medication adherence, quality of life, and physical health status among men living with HIV/AIDS. He currently also leads a study evaluating immune responses to a stress reactivity task among older men living with HIV/AIDS.

Dr. Penedo is a member of several professional societies including the American Psychological Association, Society of Behavioral Medicine, the American Psychosomatic Society, and the Gerontological Society of America. He currently serves on several editorial boards of major journals, including *Psychological Bulleting* and *Psychology and Health* and is an Associate Editor for the *Journal of Consulting and Clinical Psychology*. In 2005 he received the Early Career Award from the Society of Behavioral Medicine and is a past recipient of the Early Career Award from the International Society of Behavioral Medicine and the Young Scholar Award from the American Psychosomatic Society.

Michael H. Antoni, Ph.D., is Professor of Psychology and Psychiatry and Behavioral Sciences at the University of Miami and Program Leader at the Sylvester Comprehensive Cancer Center, and has been a licensed psychologist in the State of Florida since 1987. Dr. Antoni leads the Biobehavioral Oncology, Epidemiology, Prevention and Control research program, which includes over 20 faculty members from the departments of Psychology, Psychiatry, Epidemiology, Medicine, and Microbiology/Immunology, working together on transdisciplinary research projects. Dr. Antoni also serves on the graduate faculty in both the Clinical Health Psychology doctoral program and the Cancer Biology doctoral program at the University of Miami.

Dr. Antoni has led multiple NIMH-funded randomized controlled trials examining the ability of group-based cognitive-behavioral stress management (CBSM) interventions to enhance psychological adjustment and modulate immune system functioning and health outcomes in HIV-infected men and women. He also serves as co-director of an NIMH pre- and post-doctoral training program in behavioral immunology and AIDS. He is also director of the National Cancer Institute (NCI)-funded Center for Psycho-Oncology Research (CPOR), one of the five mind-body centers funded by the NIH at the turn of the century. At the CPOR he directs a set of coordinated clinical trials and core laboratories that examine the effects of CBSM on psychosocial, endocrine, and immune functioning and the development of cervical carcinoma in women infected with HIV and human papillomaviruses (HPV) and on quality of life, endocrine and immune processes, and health status in women with breast cancer and men with prostate cancer. He has also served continuously as principal investigator for the past 14 years on an NCI-funded program of research in breast cancer that has demonstrated the efficacy of CBSM in three different randomized trials.

He has published over 380 journal articles, abstracts, chapters, and books in the area of stress management and health psychology, including *Cognitive-Behavioral Stress Management for Individuals Living with HIV* and *Stress Management for Women with Breast Cancer*. He is associate editor of the *International Journal of Behavioral Medicine* and *Psychology and Health* and serves on the editorial boards of *Health Psychology, Brain, Behavior and Immunity,* and *Annals of Behavioral Medicine*.

Neil Schneiderman, Ph.D., is James L. Knight Professor of Health Psychology, Psychiatry and Behavioral Sciences, and Medicine at the University of Miami. He is Director of the University's Behavioral Medicine Research Center and Director of the Division of Health Psychology in the Department of Psychology. Dr. Schneiderman is the Director of both an NIH Program Project and a Research Training Grant from the National Heart Lung and Blood Institute on biobehavioral bases of cardiovascular disease risk and management. He is also Principal Investigator of the NIH Multi-Center Hispanic Community Health Study as well as an NIMH Research Training Grant on psychoneuroimmunology and HIV/AIDS. Dr. Schneiderman has led multiple randomized controlled trials examining the effects of group-based cognitive-behavioral stress management on psychological adjustments and biological outcomes in the areas of HIV/AIDS, prostate cancer, and cardiovascular disease and has published more than 300 refereed articles. His honors include Distinguished Scientist Awards from both the American Psychological Association and the Society of Behavioral Medicine, and the Outstanding Scientific Achievement Award from the International Society of Behavioral Medicine.